M000203551

FORGIVENESS IN THE FIRST DEGREE

The True Story of a Son
Whose Father Was Murdered,
The Man Who Pulled the Trigger,
And the God Who Redeemed Them Both

Rondol Hammer and Phillip Robinson

with Margot Starbuck

FaithHappenings Publishers

Scripture references come from The Holy Bible, English Standard Version® (ESV®)
Copyright © 2001 by Crossway,
a publishing ministry of Good News Publishers.
All rights reserved.

FaithHappenings Publishers
7061 S. University Blvd., Suite 307
Centennial, CO 80122

Cover Design ©2017 FaithHappenings Publishers
Book Layout ©2013 BookDesignTemplates.com

Forgiveness in the First Degree / Rondol Hammer and Phillip Robinson. -- 1st ed.
ISBN (Softcover) 978-1-941555-36-1
This book was printed in the United States of America.

To order additional copies of this book, contact:
info@faithhappenings.com

FaithHappenings Publishers,
a division of FaithHappenings.com

ENDORSEMENTS

"When Rondol and Phillip told me their story two years ago, I told them they needed to write it down so that the world could see what confession, forgiveness and restoration looks like. In a culture where we're tempted to adopt our actions towards those who have committed crimes from "Law and Order," *Forgiveness in the First Degree* reveals the very Heart of God, calling us to extend grace to others no matter their crime. None of us desires to be remembered by what we did on our worst day. God sent Jesus so that we could find a new start every time we need it. These men live out that truth. You and I can too."

– Jim Liske, Lead Pastor at Christ Memorial Church,
Former President and CEO of Prisons Fellowship Ministries,
Chair of the Board at Crossroads Prison Ministries

"Those who have been forgiven much love much and I love stories that illustrate and remind us of the glorious extent of God's grace and forgiveness. Ron and Phillip's story is powerful and points to God's amazing grace."

– Eric Geiger, Senior Vice President at
LifeWay Christian Resources

"I started reading this book to honor my friend Phillip; I ended up reading the book to walk into the depths of God's wondrous love. I couldn't put it down.

"I have known Phillip Robinson since high school. I have seen him walk the path that he and Ron Hammer profess in the book. I knew every word he wrote was true and courageous. It minces no words, and it left me with tears running down my face and shaking my head in amazement at God's unyielding love. It also left me having to look into my own heart to face how much of me is still not in God's loving embrace. I hope that many, many others get to read this courageous work because it cannot help but change anyone who dares to read it."

– Dr. Chip Dodd, author of *Voice of the Heart*

"This is a story that you'll have to read to believe! Phillip Robinson's and Rondol Hammer's lives cross paths in an unbelievable story of murder and forgiveness. Watching the relationship form between these two men has challenged every part of my heart. I strongly encourage you to go on the journey with them, and in the process allow God to change your journey as well. If you have been hurt deeply by someone, you'll find a very real hope in the pages of this book that will help you move forward."

– Jeremy Lee, founder of www.ministrytoparents.com and co-author of *Pass It On*

"To be a Christian is to be totally forgiven! ... In *Forgiveness in the First Degree,* Phillip and Ron not only reveal for us the compelling and radical story of forgiving one who has committed a grievous sin against you, but they also show us how to forgive, love and embrace without resentment, even when it does not feel good, for the Greater Hallowing of our Father, empowered by the Spirit, so each of us will experience the Freedom from bondage the Gospel offers and delivers in Christ Jesus. This is book is right on time for the Church to read and embrace in an era when so many are in prison to anger, anxiousness and fear because of unforgiveness."

– Manny Mill, CEO for Koinonia House National Ministries and author of *Radical Redemption and Radical Prayer*

"'Truth is stranger than fiction,' said Mark Twain, 'because fiction is obliged to stick to possibilities; truth isn't.' When you read *Forgiveness in the First Degree* you will likely say that truth is more amazing than fiction when truth pertains to the mercy of God; such truth always seems too good to be true.

"This is a true account of what I call 'total forgiveness.' It is the story of a son whose father was murdered, written by his son, Phillip Robinson. It is also the written confession and testimony of the man who pulled the trigger, written by Rondol Hammer. It is the thrilling display of the grace of God who redeemed these two men and endowed them with mutual graciousness toward each other.

"A book like this does not come around every day. In fact this may be the first of a kind. It needs to be read and heard around the world. Buy it and give copies to your friends. It will bless every single person who reads it."

– R. T. Kendall, Minister, Westminster Chapel, London (1977-2002), author of *Total Forgiveness*

"The phrase 'forgive and forget' cheapens the cost of mercy. True forgiveness calls us inward to a heart which relents, 'You have harmed me and caused destruction deep in my soul. *And*. And I will no longer hold your crime against you.' Ron and Phillip have walked this truth deeper than most, and now become our guides in the way of forgiveness. Their courage and faith invite us to trade the hurt, resentment, and pride we carry for the freedom and redemption of a healed heart."

– Luke Brasel, Coauthor of *Inviting Intimacy*, Counselor, Blogger at lukebrasel.com

"This book takes the reader on a journey that begins in the deepest and darkest moment of tragedy and thoughtfully carries them through the emotional struggle that accompanies a follower of Christ when life hurts too much even to pray and when sorrow comes like an unwelcomed tidal wave. Phillip and Ron give us an honest look into their lives and the process of living again after a terrible mistake and the tragedy that followed robbed them both. Though one was deservedly incarcerated, both were held prisoner: one by justice and the other by unforgiveness. This is the story of their journey toward freedom and ultimately the most unlikely of friendships. It is a beautiful retelling of the power of God in the lives of two men who never imagined their tragic, shared experience, and the redemption that followed, would become such a dynamic testimony to the new life that confession and forgiveness can bring. Their miraculous story needs to be heard by all. There is hope and healing in these pages."

– Russ Lee, lead singer of the group NewSong

2 Corinthians 5:17–6:2

CONTENTS

1. What Was Never Meant to Be 9

2. Someone's Been Shot 16

3. Running for My Life 22

4. Numb 30

5. Convincing Denial 40

6. Pain, Rage, and an Impossible Solution 48

7. Arrested for the Murder of Frank Wayne Robinson 55

8. Justified Unforgiveness 61

9. I Deserved to Die 68

10. Vermin Deserve Extermination 74

11. Innocent or Guilty? 81

12. Hearing God's Still Small Voice 91

13. Shackled in Chains 97

14. Sentenced 111

15. Witness to Another Murder 116

16. Stuck 122

17. An Act of Mercy 128

18. Faces 134

19. Steve Didn't Do It 144

20. The Hand of My Father 151

21. Free at Last 158

22. The Hand of God Intervenes 165

23. Why I Finally Forgave Myself..173

24. My Buddy in Mountain City...180

25. Will They See I'm Different?..187

26. Time to Heal..194

27. A Traumatic Release...199

28. Brothers on a Mission 204

CHAPTER ONE

What Was Never Meant to Be

Ron, November 14, 1986

A hand reaches for the pistol I'm holding. The hammer cocks and I see a flash of light and hear a thunderous explosion as the man in front of me falls to the ground. Seeing him on the pavement, in a pool of blood, I want to scream for someone to save him, but I'm frozen. I drop to my knees, to care for him. Part of me wants to stop the bleeding and call for help. But more than that, I want to save myself. So I run. Like an animal, I choose my survival over his.

"Oh God," I beg as I run away, "Let him be okay. Please God, let him be okay..."

I would relive this moment for decades to come.

The day Wayne Robinson was shot and killed should have been like any other Friday.

My wife Sharon and I woke early to share a light breakfast and chat about the chores we were planning to do around our home over the weekend. We'd finally bought curtains for the guest bath and wanted to plant some flowers along the front walkway. We kept our voices low because my sister and her husband, who were staying with us for a few weeks, were still asleep.

Sharon and I had been happily married for six years. I was running my own successful auto repair business and we'd recently bought the home of our dreams, a three-bedroom ranch. Our driveway boasted a Corvette and a Nissan 300Z. I had a son, seven-year-old Travis, and Sharon and I were looking forward to having children together.

At twenty-seven, I felt like I had life by the tail.

After breakfast I kissed Sharon goodbye as she headed out to her accounting job at a large manufacturing company. A gust of cool November air rushed in the door as she left. The days were getting shorter and it was still dark outside. When I heard her car disappear, I headed back upstairs.

The Secret

I pulled a small bag out of a shoebox in my closet. Carefully tapping some powder onto the marbled bathroom countertop, shaping the pile with a razorblade from the medicine cabinet, I snorted a thin line of crystal meth. It was a secret I'd kept from Sharon for fifteen months.

Feeling like I could now face the day, I headed in to work. Fridays were usually busy, and as I drove the two miles to the shop, I went over the day's workload. After a brief meeting with employees, I assigned them jobs and returned to my office.

I was on the phone at 10:30 when my sister's husband, Steve, tapped on the glass. I waved him in. Steve had received a D.U.I. charge on a trip to visit us and, agreeing to attend a two-week offenders' class every evening, had returned from his home in Virginia to spend the week with us in Murfreesboro. He had one session left. I'd gotten a call the night before about a dead car that needed to be towed in to the shop and had asked Steve to pick it up for me. Handing Steve the scrap of paper where I'd written the address, I pointed at the keys to the tow truck hanging on the wall. He left before I'd finished my call.

Though neither my wife nor my sister Kathy, who was married to Steve, had any idea I was using meth, Steve knew my secret. In fact, when Steve returned to the shop about an hour later, he told me he wanted to do a line of meth with me. Because I was already worried about my dwindling supply, I explained that I'd run low and couldn't find any more. He looked disappointed.

Steve invited me to grab lunch with him at Buster's Bar and Grill, a restaurant across the parking lot from my shop. Because meth had taken my appetite, I really wasn't interested in eating. For months I'd been making excuses—to Sharon and to my mother—about why I was down to 140 pounds, often blaming my busy work schedule. But, to keep up appearances of normalcy, I'd learned to force myself to eat even when I didn't feel like it. I told Steve I had some paperwork to finish and that I'd catch up with him in a bit.

A bit after twelve thirty I wandered over to Buster's, where I spotted Steve drinking with a man I recognized but hadn't met. When I sat down in the red vinyl booth beside Steve, he introduced his friend as Monk. They'd done time together at the Rutherford County Workhouse in Murfreesboro. I reached across the table and shook Monk's hand.

The conversation quickly turned to getting high. When Monk said he could hook us up, I felt like I could breathe again. It was like Monk had an oxygen tank.

After Steve and Monk paid their tab, we walked outside.

"Can we go over to your place," Monk asked, "and I'll let you try some?"

A Dangerous Taste

As we crossed the gravel lot, I was like an excited little kid. Though I'd be happy with any hookup, I was eager to find out if the "stuff" Monk had offered would be any good.

As we got close to the shop, I could see, through the show-room window that was open, that one of my employees had a customer in the office.

Angling to the back of the lot where he'd parked, Monk opened the side door of a blue 1970 Dodge van. Wrestling a brown paper bag from under one of the seats, Monk folded it open to show us a clear bag inside with more meth than I'd ever seen. Rather than the white powder I was used to, this batch was a light brown color.

Standing in my impound lot, Monk dipped a small coke spoon into the bag and gave Steve a snort. My insides were racing. When it was my turn, I inhaled deeply. The drug kicked in immediately and I felt like a transformer was exploding in my head. I'd never experienced anything like it. I was immediately consumed with the thought of mainlining this stuff, injecting it straight into my veins.

I wanted to buy as much of it as I could.

We headed inside, just as the customer in my office was leaving. Despite the adrenaline in my system, I tried to stay calm, to signal to Monk that I could be trusted. But I was now obsessed with getting the next line. I let my shop foreman know that I'd be busy and drew the window blinds. As Steve and Monk pulled chairs up beside my desk, I locked the door. Monk laid down two tracks on my desk, one for Steve and one for me. The moment I inhaled the line was electric. I was bleeding sweat and feeling ripped.

"How much can I get for two or three hundred bucks?" I asked Monk.

"Actually," he explained, "I'm looking to unload all of it. I don't want the heat after me and I don't want to get stopped in traffic with it."

Though I couldn't imagine how much the whole bag would have cost me, I blurted, "I don't have that kind of cash."

I knew Steve didn't have it.

"Listen," Monk lowered his voice, "I know how you can get it."

Monk told us about a grocer who delivered small bills to the IGA grocery store, on Memorial Boulevard, on Fridays, just before five o'clock. He guessed the bag held $6,000 to $8,000.

"It'll be easy," Monk promised us, "to walk up to him, show him a gun, take the bag of money, and run."

"Ron can run!" Steve interrupted. "He's a quick runner. He's won lots of awards and been in races in the military."

I ignored the comment. I did love running, but had never dreamed I'd need it in a situation like this one.

To say we weren't thinking clearly was an understatement.

"If you get the bag of money," Monk negotiated, "I'll trade your bag for my bag."

Because we didn't want to be seen in our own cars, I begged Monk to drive us there, and drop us off. Maybe because he was more sober than we were, he refused. We'd have to figure out another way.

When Steve and Monk left the shop, around 1:30, my mind was buzzing. On one level I understood the foolishness of what we were about to do, but because I could no longer function without meth, my addiction stifled my better judgment. Though robbing someone at gunpoint wasn't anything I'd ever considered before, my mind was fixed only on getting the dope. Steve and I would meet up later that afternoon, do the job, and meet Monk back at my shop at 7:00 to trade a bag for a bag.

The Job

Most of my energy over the next few hours was spent trying to appear normal. High, confused, afraid, I avoided contact with others as much as possible, keeping busy in my office.

Steve called around 4:00 to suggest I meet him on Northfield Boulevard, a few miles from the shop. He'd be driving a stolen truck, he explained. Panicked, I grabbed my pistol out of a safe in the office, some coveralls, and the police scanner I used to listen for reports of wrecks.

Trying to look casual, I left in one of the shop's trucks without telling anyone, driving off as if I was grabbing a burger or making a bank run. When I got to the spot Steve had described I parked and got into the red truck he was driving.

Already running behind schedule, we drove to K-Mart and bought two ski masks. Nervous, wild-eyed, I'm sure we looked more like thieves than winter sport enthusiasts.

The traffic between the K-Mart and the IGA was heavy, and time was tight. If we missed the man with the bag of cash, we might not get another opportunity. Glancing at my watch, I noticed it was just past 4:30. We'd be cutting it close. Stuck behind a line of cars at a red light, Steve suddenly swerved off onto a service road.

"What are you doing?" I asked. "We're late already."

"We need something to calm our nerves," he explained, pulling into the parking lot of a liquor store.

Rushing in to the store, Steve emerged a few minutes later with two take-out half pints of liquor that we opened and wolfed down. I wasn't used to drinking liquor and I felt the effects immediately.

When we left the parking lot we had just minutes to get to the IGA. I wrestled into my coveralls in the front seat as Steve drove, and he stopped at an apartment building to put on his.

It was about four minutes before five when we pulled into the IGA lot where the grocer man was supposed to park, right beside the store.

The Bag

As we pulled around the corner, Steve announced, "There he is!"

We were both looking at a man in his fifties, wearing dark slacks, a white button-down shirt, a blue striped tie, and a dark jacket. He was just getting out of his car. Locking the door of a beige Olds Delta 88 with a maroon vinyl top, he was turned away from us.

Panicked, pushing my pistol across the seat toward Steve, I demanded, "Who's going to do this?! Go, go, you do it."

Steve shouted, "No, you do it, you do it! You're fast. Go, go!"

As the man turned to walk toward the store, I grabbed my gun off the seat, jumped out of the truck and ran toward him.

Terrified, I hollered instructions.

"Give me the money," I shouted, holding my pistol and inching forward toward the man, "put the bag on the ground!"

But when the man refused my order, chaos erupted.

Strong grip on my shoulder.

The man's hand reaching for my gun.

Explosion of sound.

Flash of light.

Man down.

Terror.

Run.

When time began again, I was back in the passenger seat of the stolen truck and Steve was hitting the gas as we sped away.

"Oh God," I begged, "Let him be okay. Please God, let him be okay . . ."

CHAPTER TWO

Someone's Been Shot

Phillip, November 14, 1986

Mom," I spoke into the phone, "I called to tell Dad that someone was just shot in front of the store. I need to talk to him."

I'd worked with my dad at his grocery stores since I was nine years old and, over those twenty-one years, had moved up the ranks to Assistant Manager. My father had been on vacation for a week and had just returned back to work. Around three thirty he'd gone home to have a meal and go to the bank, and I thought he'd want to know what had happened.

When I'd heard what sounded like a gunshot in front of my father's IGA store, around five fifteen on Friday evening, I ignored it. I assumed it was kids playing with firecrackers or a couple of drunk men bickering over a woman and shooting their pistols off into the air. I'd been in charge of the store over the previous week and, prepping the store for Thanksgiving, wanted to put up the final case of Candiquik I'd been stocking. But when customers and employees began to buzz that someone had been shot in the parking lot, I paused and dipped into the back office to call home to let my father know what had happened.

"Phil," my mother explained, "he's gone to the bank."

The life drained from my body.

"I'll call you back Mom," I spit out as my trembling hand fumbled to place the receiver back on the phone.

Sprinting through the store, past carts and customers and other displays, I burst through the automatic doors at the front of the store to see my dad lying on the sidewalk, just about five strides from the entrance. Blood was oozing from his side. A woman crouched beside him held his head and was using his jacket to apply pressure to the wound. His glasses had fallen off and the glass had shattered.

Though a crowd was beginning to gather, few seemed to know what to do. When a cashier assured me that she'd called 9-1-1, I dashed inside and leapt over the courtesy counter to reach the nearest phone. I had to let my mother know immediately. Because I feared my mother would be too upset to drive, I told her I was on my way to pick her up at home, just a few miles from the store.

Desperate, I fled from the explosive, life-altering chaos I could not control.

Responding

My heart was racing and my hands were still trembling as I jumped into my butterscotch-colored Pontiac Lemans. I rolled through stop signs and broke speed limits as I drove to my mom's home, my heart thumping rapidly. When I pulled into the church parking lot next to her home and found her heading to her car, I noticed her freckly tan from the Gulf Shore. I insisted she get into mine. As she did, she was full of questions.

"What happened?"

"Why would anybody do this?"

"Where was he shot?"

I couldn't answer one of her queries.

As we approached the store we could see that an ambulance and police car had arrived. We parked and rushed from the car, pushing through those who had gathered to see what was happening.

My dad was still on the ground, lying on what looked like a backboard. Pushing through the crowd, we moved to his side. An EMT, a young man with a ponytail, crouched over my dad and began to cut off the white oxford shirt that had been my dad's daily uniform as long as I could remember. Police officers instructed the crowd to move back so the paramedic had room to work. A young woman emerged from the back of the ambulance with a bag of fluids she began to administer in my dad's arm.

Pushing past the police officers, my mom fell to her knees beside her husband, stroking his arms and speaking gently to comfort him.

"I'm here, Wayne," she cooed. "You're going to be alright. You just hang in there now."

I saw my dad's head turn toward her. His lips moved, but no sound came out.

Pulsing with anxiety, I watched helplessly. Though the paramedics had slowed the bleeding with gauze, a puddle of blood stained the ground where the life had poured out of him.

When my mother stood up, a cashier from the store solemnly handed her a plastic bag containing my father's broken eyeglasses and the pen he always kept in his breast pocket. They'd both dropped to the ground when he'd fallen.

Carefully hoisting the backboard up onto a gurney, the pair swiftly loaded my father into the ambulance and instructed us to meet them at the hospital, about four miles away. As sirens blared, and lights atop the truck spun, I helped my mom back into the car and headed for Middle Tennessee Medical Center.

By the time my mother and I were walking toward the emergency room entrance, we could see that the truck still parked in the ambulance bay was already empty. Identifying ourselves at the desk, we were told that doctors were working on my father and that we should get comfortable in the waiting room. We would be alerted when there was news. After my mother completed checking my father in as a patient, she used the hospital phone to call my sister Debbie in Las Vegas.

I'd phoned my wife Susan from the store, before we'd left, barely able to speak. Despite willing myself to hold it together, I broke down in tears. As word spread, a few friends and family began to crowd the emergency room waiting area. A manager from the store spoke quietly to his wife, who worked at the hospital as a nurse's assistant. A neighbor who'd happened to be at the store offered my mother a cup of water. As word spread, the shooting was even announced at an Middle Tennessee State basketball game where my dad was a fan. Many wandered in, offering a hug or kind words. The scene, which looked like something out of a television drama, felt surreal.

Though I busied myself caring for my mother, calling Susan to report the severity of the situation, and sharing what little information we knew with loved ones, I can't remember ever feeling more lonely.

Waiting

Like so many thrust into situations we would never have chosen, I quietly begged God for mercy as we waited for news from the doctors. Cognizant of the severity of my father's injury, I asked God to guide and equip the doctors and nurses who were fighting to save his life.

Seated in a vinyl chair in the waiting room, I overheard my mother relaying to a neighbor the little she knew about the shooting. Distracted, barely hearing their words, I replayed the events of what had been a typical day at the store.

At lunchtime Susan and our sons Nathaniel, who was four, and Andrew, who was seven months, had brought me a burger and a salad from Wendy's. As I scarfed down a burger I noticed my dad, standing behind the courtesy counter, making funny faces and speaking in baby-talk to Andrew. It was obvious, to me and to others, that he delighted in his grandsons.

As I'd been powering through lunch, though, I wasn't thinking about the richness of the life I enjoyed: a beautiful supportive wife, two healthy sons, food for our table, and the opportunity to work with my dad in the business we both loved. Per usual, I was mentally reviewing the shipments we'd received that day and thinking about which boxes needed to be shelved first.

Why hadn't I appreciated the moment?

My life was full and my father's was as well. In fact, he and my mom had just returned home from a vacation in Gulf Shores, Alabama. Though they'd intended to stay longer, they'd come home a day early, arriving the previous evening. Though the beach at Gulf Shores was my dad's favorite spot on the planet, he'd often start to get itchy to return to the store when he was away for too long. So, after a short night of sleep, he'd shown up at the store early that Friday morning, and it hadn't taken him long to get back up to speed.

After being in charge for a week I was still spinning on high gear myself. Earlier in the afternoon I had nearly collided with my dad as I was hurrying to return a cart to the cart bay. Teasing, I got up in his face, feigning confrontation, and warned, "If you don't get out of my way, I'll send you back to vacation!"

"Sounds good to me!" he retorted, playfully. "I'm ready to go!"

As my dad now hung in the balance between life and death, the ominous words echoed in my mind. He was only fifty-five. He *wasn't* ready to go.

I wasn't ready for him to go.

Gone

Less than forty-five minutes after we'd arrived at the hospital, a nurse escorted my mother and me back to the family counseling room. As if wading through a morass that smelled of hospital sanitizer, we went dutifully, knowing in our hearts what a doctor was about to tell us. The doctor who'd fought to save my father's life told us that the wound he'd suffered was too severe.

My father had died at 6:15 p.m., November 14, 1986.

When the nurse who'd stood respectfully by the doctor's side asked if we wanted to see my father's body, my mother didn't hesitate.

"No," she spoke firmly, "he's not here anymore."

I knew my mother still lived with haunting images of her own father's difficult death and in that moment she knew, instinctively, that she didn't need to see the bloodied corpse of the man she loved.

Somehow, in the wake of the doctor and nurse's sincere condolences, we stood and walked back down the hallway toward the crowd that had gathered. With my arm around her shoulders, I steered my mother toward the exit. Those present seemed to understand our solemn march, and let us pass through without a barrage of questions. As I made eye contact with my mother's neighbor, I signaled with the slightest tip of my head that my father had not made it. She rushed over to hug my mother.

I mumbled rotely, politely, to the group, "Thanks for coming here. We're going home now."

When my father had been shot, around five o'clock, the sun had already begun to dip behind the horizon. And when we stepped through the door of the emergency room, a deep darkness had descended on the day.

On November 14, 1986, my dad did not go home to his bride.

CHAPTER THREE

Running for My Life

Ron, November 14, 1986

As blood spilled from the man lying on the ground, whose name I did not know, I jumped in the truck and Steve sped off behind the IGA. He'd barely made it out of the store's parking lot when we jerked forward and the truck came to a dead stop. The hotwire he'd used had failed.

"Run! Run!" Steve yelled, jumping out of the truck and taking off on foot.

Desperate, with no communication between us, Steve and I took off running in different directions. Though I had no memory of ever grabbing the bag of money, I looked down and saw it in my hand. The canvas drawstring bag read, "First Tennessee National Bank."

Like the wild animals I'd seen on television being pursued by a pack of lions or tigers, I ran as fast as I could through a field, struggling against briars and thick bushes. After racing at full speed for about a quarter mile, I stumbled and fell down into a thicket of bushes. Looking toward the heavens for help, I saw a disturbed roost of blackbirds flood the darkening sky. Hidden from view, panicked, I began to vomit.

Desperate Escape

Ripping off my black ski mask, I wrapped the gun inside it and buried it under a patch of bushes. Though the air was cool and it was raining lightly, I was burning up.

When the mask and pistol were concealed, I started running through the field again, still gripping the bag of money because I didn't know what else to do with it. After about a half mile, I skidded down a steep drainage ditch, close to a road. The ground was muddy and I started digging back the soft mud and dirt, creating a hole big enough for the bag. I wasn't looking for landmarks that would help me return and find it later because I had no plan to come back for the money. I simply wanted to get rid of the remaining evidence of our crime. When the hole was big enough, I dropped the bag in, covered it with mud, and climbed back up the bank. Night had fallen and it was becoming more difficult to find my footing in the open field.

Spotting the lights of a new subdivision of houses across the road, I crossed over and ran through the neighborhood, trying to figure out where I was. Wearing coveralls caked in mud, I'm sure I was an offensive sight to the residents pulling into their driveways after work. But all I could think about was making it to safety.

When I reached a river, and finally knew where I was, I began to follow the edge of the Stones River. I traveled south on a hunch that it would eventually lead me back to my shop.

Tracing the path of the river for several miles, I continued to beg God for the wounded man to live. I also dreamed up scenarios in which Steve and I would not be caught.

After about twenty minutes, I arrived at a beautiful spot where I'd fished several times. It wasn't far from my shop. I climbed up the embankment until I reached the fence around the impound lot of my business. Knowing the employees had locked up and gone home, I used the keys in my pocket to enter through a back door.

Stepping into one of the restrooms, looking in the mirror, I didn't recognize the person looking back. Though the bony features were familiar, the person I saw was someone other than who I knew I really was.

It would be many years before I'd meet that person again.

Before driving home I washed up and changed into clean clothes.

A Call From Steve

As I pulled onto our street, my sister Kathy drove past me, leaving the neighborhood. I lifted my hand in an obligatory wave, grateful to have one less person to face when I got home. As I walked in the door, the phone rang. Sharon answered it and then handed it to me. It was Steve.

Police had spotted Steve walking down the street wearing pants wet up past the knees. When he went into a pizza parlor to get some food, they'd stopped him and asked him to come downtown for questioning. At the station they allowed him to call me to ask for a change of clothes.

"Hey man, this is Steve. I need a favor," he began.

The tone of his voice told me our conversation wasn't private.

"Yeah," I replied coolly, "what's up?"

"There's been some kind of mix-up and I'm down at the police station." He asked, "Can you bring me a change of clothes?"

The police station?! My nerves were shot and I wasn't convinced I could pull it off. But, in case someone else was listening to our call, I answered in the affirmative.

"Sure, no problem."

"Thanks," Steve answered.

I hung up the phone, knowing that we'd have to figure out our next move later.

I glanced at the clock in the kitchen. It was almost seven thirty. I'd sobered up from the alcohol but I needed a hit of meth if I was to pull myself together and quiet my nerves enough to walk into the police station.

Before grabbing some of Steve's clothes, I went upstairs and dug under our queen-size mattress. I knew Sharon couldn't lift it alone and it was one of the places I used to hide small bags of drugs. Pulling out a baggie, I tapped some meth out onto our bathroom counter and inhaled deeply. The hit gave me the synthetic confidence I needed to be able to go down to the police station.

Jumping in my Corvette, I drove downtown, hoping I could leave the sack of clothes at the front desk and hurry out. But when I explained that I'd brought clothes for my brother-in-law, I was sent down the hall to the room where Steve was being questioned.

A detective, spotting me through the glass, waved me in. He was tall, with thinning brown hair. The other detective was stocky, about my height, with thick dark hair.

"I'm just dropping off some clothes," I offered, handing them to Steve and pivoting to leave.

"Let's chat," the officer invited.

The officer explained to me that there had been an "incident" at the IGA grocery store and that they'd been asking Steve a few questions about it.

I felt the eyes of the two detectives on me, reading my response.

"We just found out," one added, "that the man who was shot has died."

Nausea returned.

"I'm so sorry to hear that," I said, using the good manners my mother had taught me. I wasn't feigning compassion, though; it was genuine. I willed myself to behave like someone who was innocent and believed I was fooling them.

I believed I'd succeeded.

When the detectives allowed me to go, while they kept questioning Steve, I was relieved to leave the station and hurry home.

Safe at Home

On the drive, my heart raced. Because my mind kept returning to the haunting image of the grocer lying on the ground, I couldn't think clearly. The past that I couldn't change, and the future I feared would result from it, kept colliding in my heart and mind.

When I arrived home, Sharon and Kathy were eager to hear what had happened. I casually mentioned that Steve had been picked up but that it was probably just a case of mistaken identity. Kathy seemed to buy the story, but Sharon's face showed concern. Steve had had brushes with the law before, and had been to prison twice. I assured them both that it was probably nothing. I then reported that I wasn't feeling well and that I needed to lie down. When Sharon asked if she could help I assured her I just needed rest.

That evening, and for countless more to come, refreshing rest would elude me. My mind raced. Why wasn't Steve back? What had he told them? Had he implicated me? Should I run? Should I tell Sharon what happened? My mind scrolled through a series of horrible outcomes. Finally I grabbed a cup of water from the bedside table and threw back a handful of Valiums. Within minutes I was unconscious.

I awoke to see Sharon's face just inches from my own.

"Ronnie, wake up," she pleaded. She looked concerned.

"Honey, the police brought Steve home," she told me in a quiet tone. Then, with some confusion in her voice, she said, "They want to talk to *you*."

"Me?" I asked, groggily. I pretended to be as confused as she was. "Okay, I'll see what they want."

My heart pounded in my chest. Though I wanted to bolt, I took a deep breath, got up and walked downstairs. The two detectives I'd met earlier were standing in the front foyer of my home.

"Good evening officers," I began, "what can I do for you?"

One of the detectives answered, "We just gave your brother-in-law a ride home, and wanted to make sure you'd gotten home safely as well."

Trying to act as natural as possible, I replied, "Yes, I'm fine. Thanks for bringing him home, officers."

When the police officers left, Steve and Kathy retired to the guest bedroom and Sharon and I prepared to go upstairs to ours. Before turning off the lights to walk upstairs, Steve and I exchanged concerned glances. Sharon was full of questions and I reassured her that there'd simply been a mistake.

As far as she knew, she had no reason not to believe me.

After I heard her peaceful breathing as she slept beside me, I continued to wrestle with the unbearable thought that I'd taken a human life—something I'd not even done when I'd served with the Marines in Vietnam at the end of the war. It seemed to me that the best course of action would be to go to the police and tell them the truth: *it had been an accident.* Because I wasn't really a *killer*, I felt there must be a way that we could set things straight. I begged God to save me from the consequences of my actions.

Conspiring

The next morning was Saturday. When I woke up, the clock read 3:45 a.m. My first thought was, "Oh God, let last night be a horrible nightmare." As I realized that nightmare was now my life, I didn't want to be alive. Though it was hard to think clearly, the thought that kept forcing its way back into my mind was that I should go to the police, tell them it was an accident, and that I never meant to hurt anyone.

At around 5:30 a.m. I slipped out of bed as Sharon slept, hoping to speak to Steve privately, to get our stories straight. Steve and I had grown up together in Virginia, and often when I hung out with him I'd get into things I'd later regret. Still, because Steve had been to prison a few times before, I looked to him for advice.

Steve was at the kitchen bar drinking a Scotch.

"What do you think we should do?" I whispered nervously.

"What do you mean, 'What should we do?'" he asked, as if it had been the most foolish question in the world.

"I mean," I explained, "should we just go back to the police station and tell them it was an accident? Maybe they'd be more lenient if we confessed and told them it was an accident."

Steve's expression told me the answer before he spoke.

"No," he said firmly, "we not goin' to do that. We told them that we weren't anyplace near the IGA. You were at work and I was runnin' errands for you."

"What do you mean *we*?" I asked dubiously. When I dropped off Steve's clothes at the police station I'd been careful not to say anything.

"Last night, fool," Steve chided, "when the cops brought me back here."

The last thing I remembered from the previous evening was telling Sharon I wasn't feeling well and taking Valium to sleep.

"I don't remember them being here. What did I say?!" I begged, worried I would have spilled the beans.

"You did fine," Steve assured me.

"But what if people saw us?" I asked.

"We had them masks on," he retorted, brusquely. "Just stay cool."

Cool? I couldn't remember Friday night and I couldn't forget Friday afternoon. I wasn't sure I could pull off "cool."

Steve could sense I wasn't fully committed to our story.

Looking me straight in the eyes, he instructed, "Deny everything. They don't got anything on us. If they did, they would have arrested us by now."

"Okay," I answered weakly.

But one question continued to bother me.

"The chamber was empty when I checked it," I told Steve. "Where did that round come from?"

"Well it *wasn't* empty," he lashed back.

It had been, though. I'd been raised to handle guns with respect and I understood the power of a handgun.

The chamber had been empty.

Hadn't it?

CHAPTER FOUR

Numb

Phillip, November 17, 1986

As I helped my mom into my car in the parking lot of the Middle Tennessee Medical Center emergency room, I couldn't bear to think of leaving her in the empty home she'd shared with my dad for thirty-five years. Although my mother insisted she'd be fine staying at home, I wanted us both to be near my wife and boys. I drove her to her house so she could make some phone calls before we drove to my house.

The first thing my mom did when she stepped in the door was to call her sister, Elise, who lived in Nashville. She wanted to share what had happened and to ask Elise to deliver the news, personally, to their mother. No answer. After gathering her belongings to stay at my house, and making several other difficult phone calls, she tried again. Unable to reach Elise, my mother finally left a message for her sister to call immediately. Her sister, who'd been out for the evening, returned the call just as my mother was stepping out the door, a few minutes before nine o'clock. The timing was perfect because my mother knew that her own mother would hear about the shooting on the ten o'clock news, and wanted to prevent it.

I heard her instructing her sister, "Wayne was robbed and murdered tonight, and I'm getting ready to go to Phillip's now. I want you to get mother on the phone and keep her occupied."

And that's exactly what her sister Elise did that night, making small talk until 10:30 when the news ended. The next morning my aunt visited my grandmother and broke the news face to face.

Drama Lovers

Susan met me at the door with a silent hug. Wrapping her arm around my mother, she led her to the living room and sat down with her. I heated up some chili leftover from the dinner we'd planned to have with Susan's sister, Karen.

Hearing that Granny was coming over, the boys had stayed up to see her. Eager to visit, our blissfully oblivious Andrew crawled up into his Granny's lap. I tried to distract him, but my mother said she wanted to read him a story. Nathaniel wriggled down and ran to get *Good Night Moon* from his bedroom. Though she soldiered through it like a champion, I heard her voice falter as she read, "Goodnight comb, goodnight brush. Goodnight nobody, goodnight mush."

Goodnight nobody.

I wondered if we were thinking the same thing: the previous night, after their drive home from Alabama, was the last time she'd ever say goodnight to my father.

As I glanced out the front window into the night, I noticed the heavy darkness that had settled in my heart. The sadness, loneliness, anger and fear stung with an intensity I'd never felt before.

On this journey I had not chosen, they would be some of my closest companions.

Making Arrangements

Saturday morning my mother and I visited Woodfin funeral home to make arrangements for my father's service.

The Woodfin family treated us with kindness and gentleness, leading us through a series of choices as we sat in red plush chairs in their office. Though we were able to select a casket and choose some hymns, we were informed that the exact time of the visitation and the service would be on hold until the medical examiner completed his autopsy and released my father's body to Woodfin's. This would be the first of many moments that would remind me that the State of Tennessee was now in charge of many of the broken pieces of this new life that had been thrust upon us.

The last time I'd darkened the doors of Woodfin's Funeral Home was two years earlier, when my father had buried his mother. Like my own mother, she'd been an active employee at the market my father had inherited from his own father, who'd already passed. After her funeral our family gathered for lunch at Captain D's, which had been one of my grandmother's favorite restaurants. I remember being impressed by my dad's steadfastness as I'd watched him manage all the arrangements during that difficult time.

"Dad," I'd offered, pausing from the fried shrimp I was eating, and looking him square in the eye as he sat beside my mother, "I hope I can conduct myself with the same strength and dignity that you have when my time comes to grieve the death of one of you."

I imagined that time being several decades in the future.

Tears welled up in his eyes as he confessed, "The hardest thing to do was to terminate her from the payroll."

Now, as my mom told Mr. Woodfin what kind of service she'd like, my mind wandered back to that moment two years earlier. I realized that, as the store's assistant manager, I'd have to instruct our payroll company to "terminate" my dad from the payroll. I fought back tears at the thought of it.

Not long after my mom and I returned to her house, we received a phone call from Woodfin's letting us know that my father's body had been released into their care. Visitation, we were informed, would be the following day, Sunday, and my father's funeral service would be held on Monday.

Base of Operations

The day after my father's murder, my mother's home became both our base of family operations and also a landing place for fellow mourners. What I'd noticed before in times of tragedy, that there are three kinds of people who show up, proved more than true that weekend.

First, there were the people you expect to be present. My sister Debbie flew in from Las Vegas where her husband was stationed with the military. My mom's sisters, Julianne and Elise, came. My father's brother and his family, who also lived locally, came to lend their support.

Second, people showed up who weren't expected, but are welcomed with gratitude. Mike Thomas, a former associate pastor from a church Susan and I attended, was one of those. His unanticipated presence, and prayer with our family, meant the world to me.

Finally, there were the busybodies. One Geico commercial features a lady who shows up at the door with a pie to welcome a new neighbor, solely for the purpose of snooping. We had those, too. Some of the folks milling about my mother's living room—tittering about rumors they'd heard, speculating what race the criminals had been, repeating what the morning paper had reported—were like bees drawn to a hive of drama.

As I paused near the living room to sample food that had been delivered by neighbors and church members, I overheard my mother describing details from her recent vacation to a few of her friends.

"On our way home from the Gulf Shore we were driving through Birmingham," she reported, "when we heard on the radio that a retail business owner had been shot and killed while returning from the bank."

We'd been so consumed with other details that my mother had not shared this with me since her return.

She continued, "I have *always* told Wayne that it's not safe. Even walking the short distance between his car and the store with the bank bag is a risk."

"And what did he say?" a friend gently asked.

My mother answered wryly, "He said he had a *plan*."

The word "plan" dripped off her lips with a mixture of frustration and sad resignation.

She added, "He told me that if anyone ever tried to rob him, he'd throw the bank bag up on top of the store roof."

Silently digesting the information, her friends from church nodded their heads in unison.

As Susan signaled me to greet a guest who'd just arrived, I wondered why my father hadn't executed the plan.

Would he still be alive if he had?

Making Meaning

That night my mother insisted on sleeping at her own home. Because Debbie had arrived, I agreed. When I finally got back to my house, long after Susan had put our boys down to bed, I slipped into the bedroom we shared. Reaching for the beige phone that sat on the nightstand beside our bed, I dialed the number of my pastor. I shared with him that God had revealed a word to me. I knew that folks in our town and in our congregation were horrified and gripped by the story of my dad's murder. I'd heard some of them wondering aloud what kind of monsters living among us could commit such an atrocity. As I'd been listening to loved ones and strangers reacting to my father's murder, I'd heard a bitter edge of judgment in so many voices. And God had been reminding my own heart that sin is sin. Yes, murder is a sin, I reasoned, but lying is too. It all has to be covered by God's grace. I asked the pastor if I could share what I was learning with the congregation the next morning.

Though kind, his answer was *no*.

Recognizing how emotionally charged my presence would be, and how disruptive, he gently suggested that I didn't need to be at church. Grudgingly, I obliged.

He'd been gone only a day, and I wanted to manage the way people made meaning of my father's death. The way I functioned in the wake of my father's death was the way generations of grocery men in my family had functioned before me: I *managed*. To be fair, it's what I'd been born and bred to do. I managed my mother, being the ever-present dutiful son at her side. I managed my emotions, staying too busy to allow them expression. And now I even wanted to manage the hearts of the people in my congregation. It was a lot easier for me to testify that God was in the business of redeeming sinful hearts than it would have been to face and to feel the emotional impact of the very particular sin of one man who still roamed free.

If I'd been emotionally healthy enough to experience the feelings inside me, rather than stuffing them down, I probably would have seethed with anger. I would have pined with loneliness. I would have trembled in fear. And I certainly would have collapsed under the guilt I felt for dashing away from the scene where my father lay dying to fetch my mother. I knew there were neighbors who easily could have whisked her to the store. But of course, if I was honest, I preferred the predictability of duty to the terror of standing helplessly nearby while my father's life drained away on the pavement.

Rather than face any of those feelings, I managed.

Sunday

The headline of Sunday's edition of the *Daily News Journal* trumpeted, "Police find evidence in IGA Slaying." After a round-the-clock search that originated in front of the store and fanned out into the surrounding area, officers and detectives had recovered a ski mask near a creek behind nearby apartments. No money or gun had been found.

Inside the paper was an editorial about my father's impact on our community, extolling his generosity in supporting a local Christian school, as well as local youth sports teams, and his church. The review was like an anchor marking the moment that changed my life.

In addition to trumpeting his virtues, the piece also grieved his senseless death.

The death of such a man as Mr. Robinson diminishes a community under any circumstance, but to have him taken in such a brutal, senseless manner makes his passing a deep tragedy. And, certainly it is a tragedy when criminal vermin can steal the life of such a fine, well-liked person, a businessman who prospered and thereby caused others to prosper with him, a family man in the best traditional sense and a devout man who practiced his religion.

The article's testimony to my father's impact in the community was deeply meaningful for me. But of all that was being written about my father's death and the ongoing investigation, two words would lodge in my heart and mind, gripping me for the season to come: *criminal vermin.*

Visitation

The store had remained closed during the funeral service, and not a moment longer—as my dad would have wanted! Sunday morning my mother went early to the store, to show Uncle Woody's wife Jane what she needed to do in the office. I'd always known my mother to be a strong woman, and she was characteristically sturdy during those difficult days.

My mom and sister and I arrived at Woodfin's at eight forty-five on Sunday morning for visitation. My father's casket was positioned at the front of the room. As we waited in a private office for the visitation to begin, the funeral director remarked to my sister what a nice tan dad had, as he'd just returned from

Gulf Shores. His joyful days on the beach butted absurdly against his senseless death. Our father was dressed in his best suit and had been adorned with glasses he hated. His most recent vision prescription had been for bifocals and, frustrated with the steep learning curve, he'd refused to wear them. Instead, he quickly returned to wearing his old glasses with the outdated prescription. Because those glasses were shattered when he fell to the ground after being shot, we had given the funeral director his new pair of bifocals. Though there was nothing for him to see, the irony still would have irked him.

We began receiving visitors at nine in the morning. People heading to church or driving home after worship stopped to pay their respects to the man the morning paper had described as "the type of man for whom the term 'pillar of the community' was coined." Because the funeral home was just two blocks from my church, folks flooded Woodfin's after church let out.

The day felt both physically and emotionally grueling. Almost two thousand people streamed through Woodfin's to express their condolences to my family. Many of those who'd come that day introduced themselves as former employees, most naming dad as their first employer. These women and men who'd gone on to excel in fields that included law, banking, retail, and education raved about the positive impact he'd had in their lives. Other mourners were from my parents' small church and hundreds flowed over from my congregation.

Dutiful, I did the job that was expected of me that day, receiving and extending condolences from loved ones and strangers. Throughout the day I noticed that several salesmen and employees from the store were so emotionally distraught that they could hardly speak.

"Hmm," I mused to myself, "I'm doing better with this than they are."

It would be years before I realized I was not.

Everyone was curious to know what investigators were finding in their investigation. Throughout the day I heard myself repeating the same snippets of the story ad nauseam.

"My parents had returned early from vacation . . ."

"On Fridays we try to have enough cash on hand to cash paychecks all weekend . . ."

"I made Thursday's bank run and should have made this one . . ."

It should have been me. If my parents had spent the final night of their vacation in Alabama, the way they'd planned, on Friday evening I would have been getting out of my car, after making the bank run.

In the greatest act of kindness I experienced that day, among so many loving gestures and condolences, Woodfin's closed their doors at eight o'clock.

Monday Morning

Our family gathered together at Woodfin's on Monday morning. My mother's mother was distraught about her daughter's loss. As we waited for the service to begin, my mother firmly assured her, "Mother, I'll be alright. We have to do the best we can and go on." Apparently I'd inherited my "Keep Calm and Carry On" management style from my mother as well as my father.

Just before the funeral service began, staff at Woodfin's offered our immediate family the opportunity for one final viewing before the casket was shuffled out of view to be closed for the final time. From the parlor where we'd gathered privately that morning, we were escorted to the front of several hundred people who'd filled the chapel to capacity. Hundreds more were packed in other rooms and even outside. As we gathered around the casket, my mother stood closest to my father's head and I was standing near his feet. Tearless, empty from crying privately over the previous days, I felt dry inside. But all of a sudden my right foot began to stomp the floor, about half a dozen times. Though some attendees thought I was kicking the casket, my foot was slamming against the ground, seemingly of its own volition. It was as if all the emotion I'd been stuffing all weekend—as I managed my family, and managed visitors, and managed myself—demanded acknowledgement and came rocketing out of my right foot.

The service began promptly at 10:30 a.m. Because my parents' pastor, H.C. Wakefield, was so shaken by my father's death, I asked my own pastor, Joel Wood, to participate in the service as well. I also recruited musical talent, a pianist and vocal soloist, from my church. My mom had chosen two of my dad's favorite hymns: *Amazing Grace* and *Victory in Jesus.*

Whatever words of comfort and grace either man spoke that day were lost on me. I was numb. I know that Pastor Wakefield preached about the saving grace of Jesus Christ, and of my father's trust in him, but most of the service was a blur.

At the conclusion of the service we were escorted into a procession of vehicles that included a hearse carrying my father's body, and we slowly made our way toward Roselawn Cemetery. As I stared out the window at familiar businesses and landscape, I thought about the secure hope I have in God. Almost against my will, though, my mind kept returning to a more fragile hope: I wanted the police to arrest the men who'd caused my family so much pain.

CHAPTER FIVE

Convincing Denial

Ron, November 17, 1986

The morning following the murder, after Steve and I agreed to play it cool, I left for work in my black Corvette. Saturdays were some of our busiest days at the shop and I was glad for the distraction work would provide. I was less than a mile from home, though, when I began to cry uncontrollably. Unable to see through my tears, I pulled over to the side of the road and sobbed like a child. I couldn't bear the weight of knowing I'd taken a man's life, and I had to come clean. I made up my mind in that moment that I would drive directly to the police station.

When I approached the police station, I slowed my car as I neared the driveway to the parking lot. I wanted to stop. I wanted to go inside. I wanted to confess. But my car never slowed to a stop. Without ever consciously deciding to, I drove right past the station and headed toward my shop.

When I arrived at the garage I went inside my office and drew the blinds. Then I carefully pulled back a piece of carpet where I'd hidden my last bag of meth. Like any addict, I convinced myself that it would help me get my head straight so I could decide what to do. I genuinely believed it would "help." Once I was high, full of confidence, thoughts about confessing to police dissipated. Chemically emboldened, I believed that I could lie my way out of trouble and, in time, it would all go away.

I unfolded the *Daily News Journal* I'd taken from my front porch that morning. I learned that the name of the man who'd died was Frank Wayne Robinson. The front-page story also reported that police had discovered Steve's black facemask. My mind continued to race.

Were my fingerprints in the truck? Would they discover the gun or the money?

Should I confess to Sharon?

Should I ignore Steve's advice and go back to the station and turn myself in? Wouldn't the police be lenient when I explained it was an accident?

Should I make a run for it before the police could find any more evidence?

Although I suspected that Steve wasn't the wisest counsel, I had no idea who to turn to.

All my employees and customers that morning were buzzing about the IGA shooting.

"I think the truck was hotwired."

"You think they's from 'round here?"

"My neighbor was shopping inside. Lots of people seen it happen."

"I heard they got away with thousands of dollars."

"What do you think, Ronnie? Who do you think done it?" one asked me.

"I don't know anything about it," I insisted, retreating to work on another customer's vehicle.

Two detectives showed up at the shop around ten thirty, asking questions of me and my employees. Knowing I was still geeking out from the line I'd done when I arrived at my office, I tried to behave as normally as possible. Thankfully, they weren't as interested in me that morning as they were in Steve.

After they'd spoken with several of us, I let them know that because it was such a full day for my employees, and because Steve wasn't working that day, I'd like them to leave.

That afternoon, with no more meth at my disposal, I scored a half-ounce of cocaine from one of the guys who worked for me. Unfortunately, the coke made me paranoid, worried that my employees had given detectives a reason to suspect me. Throughout the afternoon I'd breathe short prayers to God, asking him to protect me from being charged with the crime I'd committed. Like the twisted liar I'd become, I promised God that if He'd get me out of this bind, I'd never do wrong again.

Under Scrutiny

When I arrived home that evening, there were four cars parked in front of my home. Two I didn't recognize and two were police cars. When I stepped inside I could see six or seven officers scouring my home, looking for evidence.

Panicked, defensive, I bullied the first one I encountered.

"What do you think you're doing?" I demanded.

"Mr. Hammer," he replied calmly, "your wife let us in, and we're searching your home for evidence."

I felt like a trapped animal being hunted.

"You don't have the right! Get out of my house. If you don't leave my house right now, I'll sue the entire police department."

Though I was bellowing loud enough for all of them to hear, none reacted. The invaders simply continued to search my home.

I found Sharon sitting in the living room, looking concerned.

"Don't worry babe," I assured her, "there's nothing for them to find here."

Unconcerned with my threats, the police completed their thorough search and assured me that I'd be hearing from them. When the last one left, I collapsed on the couch beside Sharon.

"What could they be looking for?" she asked. Then, lowering her voice, she asked, "Do you think it has to do with what happened at the IGA? Do you think Steve was involved?"

"How should I know," I barked back. "I don't know what they're looking for. It doesn't have anything to do with me."

I wish I could blame my abrasive reaction on my nerves that day. But interactions like those were hardly rare. Unfortunately, they'd become more and more common over the previous months as my drug use had increased. Sharon was a person generally glad to avoid conflict, but my moodiness, even before the shooting, had become difficult to dodge.

"Do you think Steve's in trouble?" she queried again.

"I don't wanna talk about it," I retorted, standing up and heading for the kitchen. As I left the room, I shouted, "I'm tired of hearing about it. I'm tired of you and everyone else pointing the finger at me."

If I'd been able to see clearly, I would have admitted I was tired of lying. I lied about work; I lied about money; I lied about my whereabouts; I lied about the reason I'd dropped thirty pounds from my already-lean frame; I lied about my agitated outbursts. Although she trusted me completely, I'd been lying to Sharon for too long. I deeply wanted to come clean, but something kept me from it.

How I Got There

Two years earlier I was busy running my successful auto repair business. One Monday I delivered a vehicle to my father, in Virginia, ten hours away. Turning right around, without any sleep, I returned to Tennessee exhausted. But because it was the evening of the local auto auction, and I needed to oversee the sale to ensure the cars I was selling fetched enough money, I went straight to the auction instead of heading home and getting some needed sleep.

As I waited for my cars to be sold, I confided in a friend who was a local car dealer that I'd been up for over twenty-four hours and was falling asleep on my feet. When he said that he had something that would give me energy, I refused.

"I'm not doing cocaine," I told him firmly.

"It's not coke," he assured me. Then he explained, "It's made in a lab and the Russians use it to keep their soldiers alert."

In fact, the drug was first manufactured in Germany in 1887. During World War II, commanders on both sides of the battle used the drug to keep their troops awake. But when it began being prescribed in the United States in the 1950s—to dieters and those battling depression—abuse quickly spread. Although I had no idea, the drug my friend was carrying around had been declared illegal in the United States in 1970. It was called methamphetamine.

Hoping that the aid that helped soldiers could help me, I let him sprinkle what I believed to be something like a caffeine boost into my Mountain Dew. Within moments I experienced a feeling of stimulation through my whole body. When I went home two hours later, I was still buzzing. After lying down beside Sharon, I pretended to be asleep, but my mind was insisting that I didn't need sleep. It was the first night that I heard and obeyed the voice that ought not be trusted.

After an alert night thanks to the wonder powder, I showed up the next morning for a court appearance involving a mechanic's loan still feeling energetic. I returned to work ready to tackle the world, but by the time evening rolled around I was needing more. Before driving home I stopped by my friend's dealership to buy some.

Immediately hooked, I still had no idea that my life had taken a drastic wrong turn. I naively believed that the "energy boost" was making my life better. Yet from the moment I'd used it, the drug had more control over me than I had over it. The lying voice whispered lies in my ear, persuading me that I was invincible. In service to the meth, I began to manipulate anyone with whom I was in relationship: my wife, my family, my friends, and my employees. By the time I met Wayne Robinson in the IGA parking lot two years later, I was bitterly enslaved.

A few years earlier, I'd seen the horrifically violent movie *Scarface*, starring Al Pacino. Pacino played Cuban immigrant Vinny Montana who worked for drug dealer Frank Lopez. As Vinny hustled his way to the top, he started living large and using cocaine. I'd seen what coke had done to buddies of mine and the story that unfolded in *Scarface* rang true. Vinny Montana began to behave as if nothing could touch him. And that's exactly how I felt when I was high. I had no worries because the drugs erased them all. They numbed my mind so that I couldn't see where I'd been or where I was heading.

For Vinny Montana, for hapless friends, and now for me, there was no lord greater than the drug.

Another Chance to Confess

Day and night, my mind never stopped racing to identify a solution that would allow me to escape punishment for the crime I'd committed. The insufficient options ricocheting through my head always included escape, confession, denial, and even suicide.

Three days after the murder I left work thirty minutes early so that I could be waiting on my porch when my neighbor got home from work. Derek was a detective with the Murfreesboro Police Department and I'd spent most of the day imagining the conversation we'd have after he rumbled down his gravel driveway.

When he slammed his car door and stepped out with his briefcase I'd holler, "Hey, could I talk to you?"

Then I'd cross the street, sit beside him on his porch, and tell him the whole story. In my fantasies he'd say, "It sounds like what you're describing was an *accident*. Why don't we drive down to the station and figure this out together."

When Derek's black Mustang finally came into view and slowed to a stop in front of his garage, I felt my stomach turn. As he emerged from his car, briefcase in hand, I opened my mouth to shout out across the yard. But somewhere between gathering my resolve and trying to get Derek's attention, I became overwhelmed with emotion. As I thought about what I did, and prepared to give words to it, I became wrought with regret, grief, and sadness, unable to speak.

Desperately wanting to escape those feelings, I slipped into our garage, and found a small bag of powder I'd hidden in a box of wires I knew Sharon would never touch. After a few minutes, my negative feelings had dissipated. I even began to feel emboldened, convincing myself of what I most wanted to believe: *I'm going to beat this because they don't have anything on me.*

As the hit wore off, though, the terror returned.

Sharon was still at work when I heard Steve's truck pull up beside our house. Emerging from the garage, I wanted to catch him before he went inside where my sister Kathy was preparing dinner.

"Steve," I began, "maybe we can explain to them that it was an accident . . ."

Steely, he turned to me and said firmly, "We don't know nothing about it. If they don't bring you in, they don't have me."

"You didn't do anything but drive the truck," I reasoned with him. Crumbling under the weight of guilt, I wanted the nightmare to end, even if it meant being held responsible.

"Ronnie, I been to prison three times. They'll give me more time than they'll give you."

"But I was the one who—" I protested.

He exploded, "No!"

"Alright, alright," I backpedaled. "We'll lay low."

Though I heard the words escape my lips, I wasn't convinced.

Over the next several weeks I would continue to drive past the police station, without ever stopping. I'd try several more times to call to my neighbor Derek when he was heading out in the morning or returning home in the evenings. Each time I attempted to confess a force that felt bigger than me seemed to keep me from doing what I purposed to do. Whether it was cowardice or the drugs that had muddied my mind and kept me from doing what I knew was right, I still don't know.

I'd like to say I was concerned for the family of that grocer, that I cared about his widow or felt for his children, but I was obsessed with the survival and wellbeing of only one man: me.

CHAPTER SIX

Pain, Rage, and an Impossible Solution

Phillip; December 30, 1986

I think he knows he's supposed to say it . . ."
   "It can't be authentic . . ."
"He can't really be doing that . . ."
"He hasn't wrestled with it yet . . ."
"I think he's just wishing it . . ."

My mother and I sat side by side on her couch, incredulous at what we were seeing on the evening news. Not long after my father's murder, I'd stopped by after work to catch her up on store news and the rumors I was hearing in the community about the murder. We'd turned on the television to hear more about the murder of Mary Catherine Strobel. She was a few years older than my father and had been killed less than four weeks after he had. She'd been driving to the Sears department store, in downtown Nashville, when she was abducted and killed by a patient who'd escaped from a mental hospital. The news report we were watching was being telecast less than twenty-four hours after her body had been discovered.

What befuddled us was the posture and attitude of family members, especially her son, Father Charles, a priest with a vibrant ministry to people who were homeless in Nashville.

"The cruelty of her death," he said, "as devastating as it is, does not diminish our belief that God's forgiveness and love, as our mother showed, is the only response to the violence we know."

We were more disturbed by what he was saying than by the murder! He was throwing around the ugly "f" word that we had not dared to speak. What dignified self-respecting victim's family members would we be if we were as brazen as he was? Within hours of her body being discovered, the day after her abduction and murder, Father Charles Strobel was talking about . . . forgiveness.

We understood what it was like to be in shock. So we didn't blame him. But I'd be lying if I didn't say we pitied him a little bit. Perhaps, as a man of the cloth, he felt it was what he "should" say. I understood wanting to do the right thing and set an example for other people of faith. Or perhaps he'd shut down emotionally, and was just going through the motions to keep functioning. That could also explain the naïve rhetoric. In time, my mother and I both reasoned, he'd come to understand that extending forgiveness wasn't as simple or easy as he seemed to be suggesting.

From a posture of superiority, I pitied Charles Strobel as being naïve.

He'd learn.

Suspects Identified

Six weeks after the shooting, two men had been identified as suspects in my father's murder, though the men had not yet been taken into custody. Guy Dotson was the District Attorney, and Bill Whitesell was his assistant who would take the lead in prosecuting the case. Guy Dotson had invited our family into his office to update us on the progress of the investigation and to review the evidence that had been gathered. My mother and I sat on a couch in his office as he filled us in on the case which he told us was far from airtight.

One of the surprising weaknesses in the case, Dotson admitted, was that there had actually been too many witnesses in the IGA parking lot at five fifteen that Friday evening. Noticing the confusion on my face, Dotson began pummeling me with questions about those who'd sat around me in the waiting room, just five minutes earlier.

How many people were there?

Male or female?

How tall was the one closest to you?

What color was his hair?

Did he have a mustache?

As a people-pleasing perfectionist, I wanted nothing more than to dazzle and delight him with my answers, but instead his barrage of questions—the same kinds of questions that would be pummeled at witnesses relentlessly by criminal attorneys on the stand at trial—made me appear foolish. When he saw me begin to squirm, Dotson was clearly pleased he made his point and released me from his imaginary witness stand. He'd read the witnesses statements and he knew that the teenage bagboy loading groceries into the back of a station wagon, and the man who'd been digging through the front seat to find his wife's shopping list, and the woman helping her toddler step up onto the curb, and the woman exiting the store, had all seen and reported very different versions of the same thing.

Because the case couldn't rely on the conflicting statements of so many witnesses, which would have cast too much doubt in the minds of the jury, the State was building a case based on the evidence they'd gathered.

Dotson shared with us other evidence detectives had found. When a fellow named Steve Kyger had been spotted on foot, less than a mile from the scene of the crime, wearing pants that were wet from the knee down, patrol officers had followed him to a pizza place where they stopped him and brought him into the police station for questioning.

While in custody, a gunshot residue test revealed traces of gunpowder on his hands. This suggested he'd recently held or fired a gun.

The fingerprints of Rondol Hammer, who was the brother-in-law of Steve Kyger, were found on the ashtray of a truck which had been stolen and abandoned near the crime scene.

Hammer's fingerprints were also on a hand-held police scanner that was recovered from the truck.

A ski mask had been discovered near Sinking Creek, just four or five hundred yards from the abandoned truck. The DA also mentioned that the truck was most likely left behind because the hotwire used to steal it had come apart, causing the truck to stall out.

It seemed like plenty of evidence to us, but the DA could anticipate how the defense would press back against it. He explained that because the circumstantial evidence was so interdependent, Kyger and Hammer would need to be tried together, rather than separately. And because the gunshot residue test implicated Kyger in handling or firing a gun, he would be tried as the shooter and Hammer as the accomplice who'd driven the truck. We also learned that divers had searched the murky Stones River, behind Hammer's shop on Northwest Broad Street. There was also speculation that a third person might have carried the money across state lines into Virginia. Dotson assured us that investigators were still searching for the gun and the money.

After I dropped my mother off at her house and was driving back to the store, I saw a battered red pickup truck and wondered if it might be "the one." I began to notice men on the street who appeared to be between 5'8" and 6'2". At a stoplight I eyeballed a man who was crossing the street, and wondered if he'd ever fired a handgun. And I was keenly aware that the man who'd killed my father was still walking about in freedom.

Holidays

Per our tradition, Susan and I had taken our boys to her family's home in Chattanooga for Thanksgiving just two weeks after my father had been murdered. I'd felt lonely as I soldiered through the family gathering, but felt very grateful to be with my wife and boys.

At Christmas, when my mom joined my family for Christmas at our home, I was reminded of the previous holiday season with my dad. Every Christmas he'd prepare country ham, one of his favorite dishes, according to an ancient method that had been passed down through our family for generations. After placing the ham in a fifty-pound metal lard can with water, and bringing the water to a boil, he removed the can from the burner and wrapped it with newspapers, blankets, and quilts. After twenty-four hours the ham was fall-off-the-bone tender, just in time for our Christmas dinner. Because my dad didn't cook at home very much, I loved watching him perform the sacred family ritual. But the year we lost him, no one had it in them to cook country ham the way he had.

That night, after their bath time, we put the boys to bed. I went to bed around eleven and opened my eyes for a moment when Susan joined me around one. At three o'clock, though, I woke up and mentally began reviewing the previous six weeks. The moment my father's funeral service was over, I threw myself back into my work at the store. And I still had not dealt with the swirling chaos of emotion that had been bubbling inside me. Because I'd said the right words, prayed the right prayers, and played the part of the dutiful grieving son, no one near me knew how low I'd sunk. Lying silently beside Susan I suddenly felt utterly bereft, my heart throbbing with anger and fear. The suffering felt unbearable.

While my father lay buried in the ground, my mother slept alone in the bed she'd shared with my father for thirty-five years, and I lay seething with rage beside my wife, the men who'd robbed our family of its patriarch might have been sleeping as soundly as babies. Learning their names had put flesh on the previously vaporous villains. Kyger, the one who'd been pegged as the shooter, lived in Virginia. And his brother-in-law, who he'd been staying with in Murfreesboro, owned an automotive business in town. Day after day, while my father's business limped along, customers continued to line Hammer's greedy pockets. For all I knew, he and Kyger were enjoying the spoils of their hunt. Two men I'd never met, and never cared to meet, had invaded my heart and mind, leaving room for little else.

I wanted them dead.

As I heard Susan breathing gently beside me, I became gripped by the single compelling thought of their extinction. I blamed them for my suffering, but there was also someone else who was equally complicit. Raised in the church, I'd become a Christian as a twelve-year-old, eager to escape the fiery flames of hell. I trusted God with my salvation, and even with daily provision for my family. But how on earth could I be expected to trust God with this? After all, hadn't the Almighty one allowed this to happen in the first place? Why had he permitted this evil that impacted so many? Why had God allowed my mother to be left alone and vulnerable? I was furious that none of the unfathomable whys had answers, and I wanted to get even with God.

When I was in college I'd watched a movie with a group of guys called The Outlaw Josey Wales, starring Clint Eastwood as Wales, a humble farmer. After renegade Union soldiers knocked Wales unconscious, they murdered his wife and son. With nothing left to live for, Wales seeks revenge on the leader of the group, the man who'd raped his wife before killing her. While he's seeking revenge, the outlaw becomes a target of the Union militia and of bounty hunters hungry for the reward money his capture will bring. Toward the end of the film, townspeople tell the Texas Rangers that Josey—who'd been shot by his hunters—had been killed in Mexico. But when a wounded Josey enters the saloon, he's recognized by the Rangers' leader, named Fletcher, one of the rebels with whom Josey had served. Fletcher plays along with the story the locals had spun. But after the Rangers ride off, he announces that because he knows Wales, he didn't believe that he could have been killed as the locals had described.

Then Wales asks, "What will you do when you find him?"

Fletcher answers, "He has got the first move. I owe him that. Then I'd tell him something."

"What's that?" Wales asks.

Fletcher replies bluntly, "That the war is over."

Remembering that film, I wished the war in my heart was over. But it was just beginning. I fantasized I was Josey Wales, slowly regaining consciousness and realizing the destruction that had been wrought on my loved ones. As the clock beside our bed ticked toward four o'clock, I wanted nothing more than to exact my revenge. But how does one get even with God? My mind spun, searching for ways I could hurt God. Convinced that God hates sin, I thought about going out and getting drunk. Nope, not bad enough. I toyed with the thought of adultery, knowing it was on God's Top Ten list. But I didn't want Susan to suffer as collateral damage in my sin spree. Then I began to wonder how much damage my .22 rifle could do to the goons who'd attacked my father. I continued to cull and review my list, hoping to exact on God the kind of pain I'd suffered. And yet in no scenario did my family not get hurt in the process.

In a fit of rage I bellowed a groan of agony and hit the wall next to my bed. Susan awoke with a start and asked if I was alright. I assured her I was and sent her back to sleep.

Exhausted, knuckles throbbing, unable to invent an effective plan to hurt God without wreaking havoc on my family, I offered the whole mess—that included me—into His hands.

But I couldn't say, with any integrity, that I trusted God in that moment.

CHAPTER SEVEN

Arrested for the Murder of Frank Wayne Robinson

Ron, March 7, 1987

P ut your hands in the air!" a man in a blue suit, gun drawn, barked at me.

I looked up from my desk where I was writing an estimate for an elderly woman needing to have her car's front end repaired. I'd just penned the date, "February 4, 1987," when I was taken by surprise as three plain clothes officers appeared as if out of nowhere with their guns pointed at me.

When I dropped my pen and carefully lifted my hands over my head, another officer yelled, "Lay down on the floor. Get down!"

Obedient, terrified, I dropped from my desk chair down to my knees, and lay down on the floor, my hands touching the ground in front of my head.

Still buzzing from a fix I'd had earlier that morning, my mind bounced wildly from thought to thought. Concerns about the employees and customers witnessing my arrest, to what Sharon's reaction would be, to whether the cops would be able to tell I was high, to who could close the shop if I wasn't back by the end of the day raced in and out of my awareness.

"Put your hands behind your back!" the first cop yelled.

Another cop clicked cuffs on me and ordered me to stand.

"You have the right to remain silent . . ." he began, as he led me out of the shop.

All of my employees and the three customers in our waiting room witnessed my humiliation.

"Hey, Bobby," I shouted over my shoulder to my shop manager, "I'm gonna clear this up, but if I'm not back by close, lock up for me."

". . . you have the right to speak to an attorney, and to have an attorney present during any questioning . . ." a detective continued in a rote, lifeless voice.

As Bobby nodded silently I did what I thought an innocent person would do. Turning to the officer who seemed to be in charge, I protested my innocence.

"This is a mistake," I informed him. "You've got the wrong person!"

The officer clutching my arm continued, ". . . if you cannot afford an attorney, one will be appointed to you."

When we arrived at the squad car, one of the officers opened the door and, placing his hand on my head, shoved me into the backseat. As I pulled my feet in, the door was slammed beside me.

Instead of being taken to the Murfreesboro police department, where I'd once fantasized about sitting with an understanding detective who'd help walk me through the legal process, I was taken straight to jail. After I was fingerprinted and photographed, I was sent to a processing room and told to strip down. Once I was completely naked, an officer instructed me to raise my arms and turn around slowly. While I turned, I was sprayed with disinfectant, like I was a dirty feral cat being brought into the house. The officer handed me an orange jumpsuit and a pair of prison-issue underwear. After slipping into the outfit, feeling as if I'd donned a costume for Halloween, I was led away to a dark lonely cell.

The first few days I was in jail, my body rebelled. Craving meth, I was physically sick and exhausted, sleeping almost constantly. While most inmates in prisons have ample access to illegal drugs, there was nothing available in the jail in which I was being detained. I continued to insist on my innocence, but inside I felt ashamed and humiliated for what I had done. I was terrified of a future over which I had no control.

Three times a day, my meals were delivered by a trustee—an inmate with a good record who has the opportunity to work inside the prison. He would slide the meal under the door the way you might feed a wild animal of whom you were afraid. The trustees seemed to have the inside scoop on what was happening in the prison. About four days after I arrived the older gentleman who delivered my meal told me that Steve had been arrested in Virginia at the same time I had been arrested, and had also been charged with first-degree murder and armed robbery. Steve had been transferred to the same jail and was housed at the other end of the building.

One evening, as he slid my meal into my cell, the trustee remarked, "Son, you better get used to this. If you done what I hear you done, you'll never see freedom again. Accepting this life is about all you can do."

Accepting that the life I'd imagined for myself—one in which Sharon and I would start a family together and I'd continue to run my thriving auto repair business—was over was the last thing I was prepared to do. Instead, I started calling on God. Not the God of the Bible who redeems sinners by transforming their lives, but a god of my own making, a kind of magic genie who would do my bidding. Half of my prayers to this genie-god were desperate pleas for forgiveness. The other half of our dealings were just that: me striking deals with God, the way I might barter with a vendor or jockey to sell a used car for parts. Among the countless hollow "if you help me" pitches I made to God, some of the most well-rehearsed ones during the three weeks I was in jail were "If you get me out of this, I'll never do drugs again" and "If you get me out of this, I'll go to church from now on." I really believed I was offering God real value with those paltry offers.

In order to raise the money for bail, I sold half of my paint shop, which was a secondary business to my mechanic shop. I'd been incarcerated for twenty-two days when a desk clerk handed me the clothes I'd been wearing when my shop had been invaded. My first stop, after Sharon picked me up, was to return to my workplace. I wish I could say that I was there to oversee my affairs or check in on the rest of my employees, but I'd returned to score a hit. Given momentary freedom, given a chance to live the way I promised God I'd live if He made my troubles disappear, I chose to return to the familiarity of bondage.

Raising Bond Money

The week after I was released, Steve asked if I could help my sister raise $10,000 to get him out on bond. Because I was out, I was free to hunt for the money we'd taken during the robbery. Though it had seemed too risky to go after it in the four months since the crime, Steve's financial need propelled me to trace my escape route in search of the bank bag I'd buried.

After Sharon was fast asleep, I slipped out of bed and drove to the subdivision near the spot where I remembered hiding it, carefully parking my car in a secluded spot. I spent three hours digging through wet grass and mud, with no success. Discouraged, covered in mud and sewage water, I cleaned up at my shop before returning home, the way I'd done once before.

Several nights later, I tried searching again, but had no luck.

My third attempt to locate the bag of cash was a night with a full moon. Within about an hour I'd found the cloth bag, like a feed sack, buried under about six inches of watery black muck. The mud was soft, and digging through it was as easy as digging up fresh clay from a pond that's just been drained. After trans-porting the wet bag home in my trunk, wrapped in an old blan-ket, I hid the bag that had been buried for four months behind my garage until I could to retrieve the cash, clean it, dry it out, and use it.

Saturday morning, as soon as Sharon left for the grocery store, I fetched my treasure, spreading it out on the floor of my garage. I was crushed by what I saw. The bills were soaking wet, stained with red ink and black smudges, rotting and reeking of sewage. I'd buried the bag near a drainage ditch and the stench led me to suspect that the developers of the new subdivision had left a sewage drain open.

Suddenly, my only thought was of destroying any trace of the loot.

Having the money in my possession made me feel anxious and vulnerable. What if Sharon had returned early and walked in to the garage? What if a neighbor had stopped by for a friendly chat? What if investigators returned to search for more evidence? I was suddenly terrified of being caught with the use-less soggy paper.

Leaving the wet bills on the concrete floor, I went out to the backfield behind our home and began to put sticks and other kindling in one of the fifty-five-gallon drums I had. Though no one was interested in my Saturday morning chores, I pretended to be burning trash and limbs. Once the fire was raging, I re-turned to the garage and scraped the bag and bills off the floor. Carrying them in the towel from my trunk, eager to destroy all evidence of the blood money, I returned to the backfield and dumped the whole load in the fire. Unfortunately, the money was slow to burn, because it was so wet. Desperate to destroy any shred of evidence, I continued dousing the bonfire with lighter fluid and gas.

I knew those damp bills were blood money. I knew they were evil. I don't think I burned it because it wasn't salvageable. I probably could have cleaned and dried many of the bills. I burned it because I was racked with fear and paranoia about what I'd done. How could I have ever spent money for which I'd taken a man's life?

As I stood watching the blaze, I began to think of all the lives that had been impacted by my greed. Although I'd never met the Robinson family, I'd read the articles about the crime in the *Daily News Journal*, like the rest of the town. A woman I'd never met had been widowed. Two adult children had lost their father. Grandchildren had lost their granddaddy. And I'd also damaged my relationships with the people I love most in the world: Sharon, my mother, and my father. I was even lying to my sister, Steve's wife. As I grieved what I'd done to each one, my attention, and blame, shifted to God. *Why had He allowed this to happen? Why had he let that gun go off? Why didn't He save the man known to all as a loving father and pillar of the community?*

I was very willing to ask those hard questions of God, but unwilling to take the same hard honest look at myself.

Sweet Freedom

From the moment I was locked up, I'd been scheming to get out. Raising my bond money, which meant I'd be free to use again, had consumed all my attention. The freedom I'd bought served no one, though. In fact, if I'd been forced to stay in jail, I believe I would have confessed. Part of me wished that would have happened.

When I wasn't blaming God for my actions, I was relishing my freedom. Being back in the real world felt amazing. The three weeks I'd been locked up without meth had felt like hell. Every day since my release, each day I was "free," I continued to use. And an hour didn't go by that I did not strategize ways to ensure I'd never return to prison again. I didn't know how to achieve that, and a voice in my head insisted relentlessly that it would be better to be dead than to be thrust back behind bars.

Death had been calling for me, and I was about to reply.

CHAPTER EIGHT

Justified Unforgiveness

Phillip, April 1, 1987

After we lost my father, his brother Woody and I discovered that the health of Frank's IGA was worse than we thought. There's a very small profit margin in the grocery business and my dad had been juggling creditors to keep the store afloat. He'd been robbing Peter to pay Paul, and when he died we discovered that he owed them both.

Successfully closing a grocery store is like stacking a towering display pyramid of cans of holiday yams. It's very delicate business. My family knew the store was in the process of closing, but the customers who needed confidence that we'd have what they needed were in the dark. I wasn't thrilled about the necessary duplicity, but knew it had to be done. We slowed down on our new orders, sticking mostly to perishables. Longer-lasting stock—toilet paper, canned goods, cereals, detergents—slowly decreased. The back stockroom began to empty out. Variety started to thin. As slower moving items sold out, the reorder shelf tag was quietly removed and facings on neighboring items spread out to disguise the emptiness. Very few people knew the store itself had a rapidly diminishing shelf life.

Though I knew my uncle would make room for me at another store he operated across town, I wasn't enthused about it.

Part of me still clung to the dream of owning and operating my own store one day. And another part of me had begun to consider the possibility of going into ministry. In the months after my father's death I felt like my life was a 1,000-piece puzzle that had been tossed into the air. It would be hard enough to reassemble all those pieces, but harder still because some of the most important ones had been lost in the wind.

Unsolicited Opinions

Just as there are stages of grieving, there are also stages and seasons of forgiveness. When Steve Kyger and Rondol Hammer were arrested in February, forgiveness was not on the lips of anyone in Murfreesboro, Tennessee. My mother was a regular morning walker at the local mall. After their exercise, many of the seniors would gather in the food court to talk. After my father's murder, when my mother became a bit of a mall celebrity, many felt free to offer her their unsolicited opinions. It often seemed to me like these folks were serving or soothing themselves with their pronouncements more than they were caring for our family.

One couple sat across from her and, puffed up with anger, the husband announced, "That man ought to be hung at the courthouse."

He expressed the sentiment of many around us. Although my mother and I weren't handing out sentences, we desperately hoped that Kyger and Hammer would be convicted. With each new revelation published by the Daily News Journal, or shared with us by the District Attorney, we'd feel like that outcome was more possible or less likely. When coveralls that could be tied to Steve Kyger were discovered by detectives, our hopes soared. When the D.A. had warned us that there were too many conflicting testimonies from various witnesses, our spirits dipped. For months we rode a rollercoaster of emotion over which we had no control. We didn't even know when the trial would occur. It had been scheduled for April, but was postponed both because the local judge recused himself because he'd had business dealings with our family and also as a result of the legal maneuverings of Hammer's and Kyger's attorneys. Our only choice was to buckle our seatbelts, hold our breath, and pray for the ride to be over.

Memories

Before it was ever trendy, my mother had, for years, kept a family scrapbook. It had a shiny brown cover, and was about three inches thick, with three rings holding in laminate photo pages. Under the clingy clear plastic, she'd clipped photos of me in the local paper for high school student government or a math competition. She had saved Debbie's candy striper photos. And she had a beautiful photo from the newspaper of the ribbon-cutting ceremony when my father opened our IGA store, standing near the spot where he had died. Standing beside his own mother, my dad was beaming alongside my mother as she cut the ribbon with huge scissors.

The last entry in my mother's scrapbook before my father was killed was a full-page advertisement for the IGA that we'd run to attract customers. "We try hard to please our customers. Putting food on your table puts food on the table for four generations of Robinsons." It features a picture of my grandmother, who supported my grandfather when he opened his first grocery store during the Depression era in the early thirties, my father, myself, and my son Nathaniel, as well as my uncle Woody. The ad was in black and white, with the exception of the bright red signature IGA oval that was part of our Frank's IGA logo.

Opposite the beautiful ad, which had run about four months earlier, was the front page of the Saturday, November 15 paper, whose tall-font headline shouted, "Owner shot, killed in robbery."

For the rest of our lives, we would mark every moment of our family's history as falling either before November 14, 1986, or after it.

Not Discussed

As we waited for the trial of Kyger and Hammer to be rescheduled, my mother and I never discussed forgiveness. On one hand, it was natural that we'd not yet had that conversation. It was too soon. The wound was too fresh. We were still grieving our loss. On the other hand, as those who identified as followers of Jesus, we'd built our lives around a story that hinged entirely on forgiveness.

If you'd asked me, I would have told you that one sin was as bad as the next. It's what I'd wanted to trumpet from the podium at church the weekend my father was killed. But if you'd really pressed me, I'd be forced to confess that I believed that Jesus didn't have to spill as much blood to forgive my flimsy sins as He did to cover the weighty sins of others. Even if I'd not been able to articulate it, it's how I behaved.

Orthodoxy was harder to swallow. Forgiveness wasn't a peripheral church teaching; God's forgiveness of us, because of Jesus, was the foundation of everything we believed. If it had occurred to us that we ought to forgive the men who killed my father, we would have had no idea how to begin.

After my father was murdered, as our whole town adjusted to his absence, not a single soul broached the subject of forgiving Steve Kyger and Rondol Hammer with me or with my mother. My parents' pastor, who loved my father deeply, did not forgive the men who'd stolen his friend. My mother's neighbor also told my mother that she did not forgive the killers. My father's sister-in-law, who was married to Uncle Woody, let us know that she did not forgive them. When my mom's Uncle Richard asked me about the case, I used the language of a good southern man, and referred to Kyger and Hammer as "gentlemen."

He abruptly interrupted me saying, "They most certainly are not gentlemen!"

I reached out to two pastors at my church who both supported me, but my heart was not yet pliable. Neither man's words penetrated my posture of unforgiveness.

When we most needed a spiritual guide to show us how to forge a path toward healing, none emerged.

Other Reactions

In the beginning of April I was arranging displays of Premium Saltines when Lindy Freeman, a salesman about the age of my dad, paused from the shelf-stocking he was working on to talk to me about the case against Kyger and Hammer. Freeman, who I respected deeply, was the quintessential soft-spoken Southern gentleman. Although he'd been in and out of the store many times since my father's murder, we'd not spoken about it together.

"Your dad was a good man," he began, gently. "He didn't deserve to die like he did."

"Thank you," I said. Then, doing what I did best—tending to others' feelings at the expense of my own—I added, "He thought a lot of you."

I arranged boxes as we continued to chat about what he'd read in the paper about the upcoming trial. Before Freeman began to stock another cart of Chips Ahoys and Oreos, I noticed his face clench in a flash of uncharacteristic anger.

He remarked, "Those two represent everything that's wrong with this world: greed and violence."

"We all fall short of the glory of God, eh?" I offered.

"Well," he continued, ignoring my attempt to soften his quiet rage, "I hope they never see the light of day again."

A bit surprised and speechless, I put my head back down and continued working.

A few hours later I was walking from the customer service desk back to the office when I saw Jeff Gilbert pushing a near-empty bread rack down the bread aisle back toward the loading dock. Jeff, another salesman who was also about my father's age, gathered gossip at every store he stocked. Had my dad been living, I knew that when he saw Jeff wheel into the store he would have sidled over to him, Styrofoam cup of coffee in hand, to swap tales with him. And if my father had lived through the botched robbery, there was no question in my mind that the two of them would have used their words to shred my father's attackers.

As I glanced at the shelves Jeff had stocked as I passed by I noticed that, per his custom, he'd expanded the shelf space his own products occupied and narrowed that of his competitors. He paused to strike up a conversation, asking me what I knew about Kyger and Hammer and gladly offered up what he'd gleaned along his route. Kyger, he reported in an unforgiving tone, had been involved in the beating death of a man when he was just fourteen years old.

"If he'd stayed behind bars like he should have," Jeff chided, "I'd be talking to your dad now, instead of you."

I tried not to take that personally.

Jeff mentioned some of the dirt he'd heard about Hammer's auto shop in Murfreesboro, detailing the illegal dealings that were rumored to be happening there.

Finally, he announced of the two suspects, "They should both be hung!"

While Jeff was probably blowing off steam, rather than offering a thoughtful commentary on the laws of Tennessee, I responded by explaining that due to the nature of the case against them, the DA wouldn't be pursuing the death penalty.

"That's just not right!" he fumed, before turning abruptly to push his cart back to his truck.

As he stormed out of the store, I felt a little bit disappointed. I could see how another man would appreciate the righteous indignation of men who'd cared for his father. But I think I'd wanted these older men in the business I loved to fill the fatherly gap in my life that had been blown open by a careless angry pistol. And while I understood that their fury was fueled by their love for my dad, a part of me knew that their harsh judgment lacked the godly wisdom for which I thirsted.

At the same time, I welcomed it. Although a small part of me knew that my heart was bound by unforgiveness, which was death-dealing to me and others, I gladly received everyone else's bitter judgments as permission to cling to my own.

As I finished my work, I quietly prayed that Kyger and Hammer would both be convicted and rot in jail. Or at least until my mother was no longer living.

CHAPTER NINE

I Deserved to Die

Ron, May 18, 1987

I came home from work one spring evening to discover Sharon in our bed, weeping.

Silently, I reached for a box of tissue off the dresser.

There was no reason for me to ask her what was wrong. I already knew. Since I'd been arrested, jailed, and released, Sharon had been overwhelmed with sadness almost daily.

The week I'd been arrested in February, the *Daily News Journal* had announced, to the world:

"The three-month-long probe resulted Wednesday in the arrest of two suspects in the case. Rondol 'Ron' Hammer, 29, and Steve M. Kyger, 30, face first-degree murder, armed robbery and larceny charges. Both men remain in the County Jail in lieu of $100,000 bond."

The article also listed the name and address of my auto repair business. It described the kind of revolver that had been used. It reported that the bag contained more than $10,000 in supermarket operating funds.

Had I not burned the money, I realized, it would have been enough to get Steve out of jail.

Of course Sharon felt ashamed. While she believed in my innocence, and had been unwavering in her support of me, the experience was humiliating. Every one of her family members, neighbors, and colleagues knew that I was to be tried, along with Steve, for murder. She also felt fearful of navigating a future that didn't include me. We'd just purchased a new home, and making mortgage payments without my income would be more than Sharon could manage, financially.

Despite all the wrong I'd done, despite my consistently poor choices involving drugs, I still loved Sharon deeply. My crime, my deceit, and my secret drug use had kept me from being the kind of husband she deserved, and seeing the suffering I'd caused her drove me to an even deeper place of despair than I'd sunk to when I thought only of myself.

Unable to offer her any comfort or hope, depleted of all emotional resources myself, I handed her the box of tissues and quietly left the room to do a line of meth in the garage.

The week I'd been released from jail, a poisonous seed had been planted in my mind: *it would be better for me to be dead than to return to prison*. Being incarcerated was no life. If I had to live behind bars, which I knew I deserved, I might as well be dead. That nasty niggling voice continued to badger me, and as I saw Sharon being crushed by shame and pain that I had caused, I concluded that the only way I could make it better would be to end my life. And if I could make it look like an accident, all the better: I could provide for Sharon in my death with the insurance money she'd receive. As I awaited the further humiliation of a trial, I became obsessed with how I could end my life.

In the cover my home's garage provided, I carefully tapped out a line of meth onto my workbench. When I snorted it up off the wooden surface, I inhaled the courage I'd need to end my life.

As I worked at the shop the next day, knocking out dented fenders and spraying coats of protective lacquer, determined, I spent hours thinking about the best way to kill myself. Throughout the day I heard echoes of my mother's voice, chiding a reminder that it was a terrible sin to take one's own life. It's what she'd always raised me to believe. Well, it was also a terrible sin to take someone else's life, which I'd already done. And so I justified my plans of suicide by using the Old Testament logic of an "eye for an eye." By the end of the day, I'd convinced myself that because I'd taken the life of Wayne Robinson, I needed to die.

At about half past five, when my last employee left, I called Sharon to let her know I would be working late at the shop. I spent a few more hours working and, after doing way too much meth, I got in my Vette and headed toward Smyrna, about a dozen miles northwest of Murfreesboro. I knew there was a massive roadwork construction project on the Nashville Highway, right at the Nissan plant exit, and crews had installed a huge cement barrier blocking off one lane of traffic on the highway. The roadway that stretched for three miles in front of the barrier was straight as an arrow. I'd decided I would push my car to the limit, accelerating and hitting the barrier as fast as my Corvette would allow. I'd built it with a 450-horsepower engine and had hit speeds of over 160 miles per hour.

I was trying not to cry on the short trip to Smyrna, but unauthorized tears began to slide down my cheeks. About a mile before the exit, I pressed my foot to the gas pedal, and began to gain speed. I watched the speedometer inch past 50 mph, then 60, then 70, then 80. By the time the needle tipped past 80mph, I was crying so hard that I couldn't see the gauge anymore, and could barely see the road. As I continued to accelerate, I confessed to God that I needed Him and begged Him to forgive me for what I'd done and what I was about to do. By the time the barrier was in sight, my car was straining to reach its limit, its engine screaming for air. I headed straight for the barrier, shut my eyes, and waited for the nothingness of death.

Though my car and body should have been crumpled like tinfoil, I opened my eyes moments later to witness what seemed impossible. I immediately slowed the car to a stop on the shoulder of the road and began vomiting uncontrollably in my car.

When I stumbled out of the car to investigate why I survived the certain collision, I saw that there had been an opening in the barrier, between sections of the concrete barricade, that was eight feet wide. Beyond all reason, my Corvette, six-and-a-half feet wide, had skimmed through the narrow opening. That slim fit would have been too tricky to navigate had I been going fifteen miles per hour, but I had passed through the slim opening at one-hundred-and-fifty miles per hour with my eyes closed!

Falling to my knees on the pavement, I continued to sob, feeling keenly aware of how weak-minded and helpless I was. I simply could not account for my survival. Was I such a coward that I couldn't even take my own life? Or had God intervened to save me? Completely rattled, I was as despondent as I'd been all week for failing at the one thing that might have made others' lives better.

That night, when Sharon should have received a phone call from the Highway Patrol reporting my death, I drove home feeling defeated. I entered the house through the front door a bit after eleven and quietly climbed the stairs. After a shower, I slid into bed beside Sharon without a word. The next morning I feigned sleep when she rose and left for her job. Though she knew better than anyone how little I slept, she went along with my ruse.

Each day I bore witness to Sharon's deep grief. Without any way to comfort her, and racked by my own pain and shame, I continued to be obsessed with a compulsion to take my life.

The next Saturday evening I drove back to Smyrna, which is where my little two-seater Cherokee Piper plane was stored. I'd told Sharon I was going to take it out for a spin, knowing that when investigators would examine the shreds of wreckage in the wake of my crash, they would have no way to prove my death had not been accidental.

As I zipped over Percy Priest Lake, I eyed the dam that served as a bridge for automobiles along the northwest edge of the lake. The dam rises 130 feet high above the streambed, and is 2,716 feet wide. There was no way to miss that hulking obstacle. I envisioned smashing into it head on and dying immediately on impact. This plan was foolproof.

I'd been circling the lake at about 2,000 feet when I dropped the plane right down above the water, nearly sailing across it, so that I could impact the dam with optimal effect. With plenty of distance to reach maximum speed, I headed for the dam full throttle, shut my eyes, and made one final plea to the Almighty, begging, "God, please forgive me!"

When I felt no impact, I opened my eyes to see if I'd met my Maker without the fiery crash I'd expected. But when I opened my eyes, my plane had somehow flown over the dam and was in a steady climb.

I'd failed again.

What seemed most absurd was that I'd spent my whole life around vehicles. I knew how they were built and I understood how they worked. I'd built a career around making them work better. And yet, when I needed them to perform in a pinch, they'd betrayed me.

I had no plans to give up.

A few days later, I left the shop during lunchtime and went home when I knew Sharon would be at work. Before going inside, I gathered my 30.06 deer rifle from the garage and brought it inside our living room. I carefully removed it from its case and loaded the gun. My hands were shaking as I raised it, touching the tip of the gun to my chest. There was no way for me to cheat death this time.

Wayne Robinson had died from a gunshot wound and because I read the Bible to allow an eye to be taken for an eye, then this—a bullet through my chest—would be an even exchange.

"God, forgive me," I sobbed, as I clenched my finger to pull the trigger.

The gun fired, and by some grace that was greater than I, it did not explode through my heart the way I'd imagined it would. Instead of tearing through my heart, the 130 grain bullet shot straight through my armpit. The bullet ripped through my flannel shirt, between my arm and my ribcage, and bore through the couch and all the way through the wall behind me.

Still crying, completely undone emotionally, I dropped the gun on the floor and buried my head in my hands. The burnt skin under my arm and along my ribs throbbed. I'd made a mess of my life and I couldn't even kill myself. Because I was so despondent at that time, there was no way to see hope or meaning in my failure. I had no imagination that God could want me to live. Could want to transform me. Could want to use me.

Each time I'd attempted to take my life, I'd begged God to forgive me for what I was about to do. Never once did it occur to me to seek God's forgiveness for the looming sin I'd committed that was overshadowing all others.

CHAPTER TEN

Vermin Deserve Extermination

Phillip, September 20, 1987

The weekend of November 14, 1986, after I'd read the editorial about the loss of my father that had been printed in the Sunday edition of the *Daily News Journal*, a single word from that article lodged in my heart: *vermin*. Without ever intending to assign it to them, the word captured the way I would label the men responsible for my father's death in my mind and heart. I figured that Kyger, who'd tested positive for gun residue and had a lengthy criminal record, had killed my dad and that the other one, Hammer, had been a hapless accomplice in Kyger's scheme.

Ten months later, the vermin were finally on trial for murder. Susan was caring for Nathaniel and Andrew at home and was seven months pregnant with our third child. She chose to be absent from the courtroom because she didn't want the "enemy" knowing too much about our family. That's how vulnerable we all felt.

The day the trial began, I picked up my mom, dressed in her typical stylish way, at her home. Her brown hair was cut and curled. She wore pearls and pearl earrings, her signature neck scarf, a white sweater, and navy slacks. When we arrived at the courthouse, she waited out in the hallway because she was scheduled as the first witness and couldn't be in the courtroom until after she'd testified. I wished her well and found seats for both of us inside.

The courtroom resembled many I'd seen on television dramas. Judge Meyer, who'd been brought in from another county after the original judge had recused himself, sat high and lifted up. Twelve jurors were gathered in the juror box on the right side of the courtroom. Kyger and Hammer sat with their attorneys at a table facing the judge, and the D.A. and his assistants representing the state sat on the opposite side of the courtroom. Rows of onlookers, separated from the attorneys by a wooden partition, lined up in benches all the way to the back of the room. Fans for the home team included my extended Robinson family, friends, a store employee who'd been like a mom to my father, and even a former teacher of mine whose daughter had been murdered. The D.A. had advised us not to look at the "away" team that included Hammer's mother and sisters, from Virginia, as well as friends and employees who were local to Murfreesboro. The courtroom was packed, with people even standing in the hallway with the reporters who'd come to cover the trial. Defense attorneys had argued that because of the media coverage, and my father being a high-profile member of the community, it would be impossible to find an impartial jury in Rutherford County. Ultimately, Judge Meyer concluded that while there was a general knowledge about the case, most of the jurors had no specific recollection as to the details that had been shared in the media. The defense's greatest concern stemmed from a newspaper article claiming that, at fourteen, Kyger had been convicted of helping another person beat a man to death. And though it hadn't made the papers, Kyger and Hammer had both been charged and convicted of burglary and attempted grand larceny in a 1980 break-in of another IGA supermarket in Shenandoah, Virginia.

In his opening statements, Assistant District Attorney Bill Whitesell advised the jury that although they were sure to hear some discrepancies in the eyewitness accounts, the trail of evidence all pointed to Kyger and Hammer as the men who robbed and shot Wayne Robinson. He identified Kyger as the shooter and underscored that Hammer, who'd driven the truck, was no less guilty.

The first witness called to the stand was my mother, since a murder case depends on proving that a person was alive. When a bailiff opened the door to usher her into the courtroom she kept her head high. Although Whitesell had advised her not to look at the defendants, she looked straight at them when she testified. She testified that my father had come home around 3:30 p.m. to eat an early supper before heading back to the store around 4:30 to make the final bank run of the day.

Whitesell asked my mother, "What was his condition at the time he was at home?"

"He was in great shape," she answered, looking a bit more relaxed. "He'd just seen his four-year-old and baby grandsons at the store, and he was telling me all about that."

I felt a bittersweet pang in my heart as I realized that his last conversation with my mother had been about my sons Nathaniel and Andrew. She continued to describe the call she got from me around 5:20 p.m. and the final minutes she'd shared with her husband on the sidewalk of his store before the paramedics loaded him into the ambulance.

After the D.A. thanked her, she stepped down from the stand and joined our family, tucking herself between Debbie and me. As the next witness was being called to the stand, I gave her hand a squeeze to let her know she'd done great.

Testimony

The next witness was the bank teller who serviced the store's account. She described the cloth bank bag she'd handed my father, as well as how many fifties, twenties, tens, fives, ones, and coins were inside. They tallied $9,561.68.

Because there'd been a light rain prior to my father's return from the bank, an off-duty sheriff's deputy reported dry spots on the pavement near my father's beige and maroon four-door 1981 Olds Delta 88.

A sack boy returning to the store after helping a customer load groceries into her car had seen two men in ski masks, and reported that the shorter, stockier one had shot the gun after Mr. Robinson jerked back when the money bag had been grabbed.

I felt like the wind had been knocked out of me when a nurse who'd been shopping, and had rushed outside to comfort my dad, had reported, "I could tell he was bleeding out."

Hollis McCrary testified that his truck had been stolen from behind the Northfield Lodge apartment complex. He refuted the defense's lie that Hammer's fingerprints were inside because he'd worked on the vehicle in his shop.

Two more witnesses testified that the red pickup had come to a stop in a field off the road behind the store before two men matching the description of the masked robbers fled in different directions.

A woman from Virginia testified that she'd loaned a pair of her work overalls, from a chicken processing plant, to Kyger. Her name had been written in them, in black Sharpie marker. They were the ones that had been recovered by investigators near Sinking Creek.

Then law enforcement professionals testified to the veracity of details that had been reported in the paper: spotting Kyger walking without a jacket not far from my parents' home, the discovery of the dark blue ski mask and overalls, Hammer's fingerprints on the police scanner and truck ashtray, and that the ashtray print was positioned as if Hammer had been driving.

Confident, the prosecution rested their case after two and a half days of testimony. Because Kyger and Hammer were being tried together, both defense teams then appealed to Judge Meyer with severance motions, claiming that the State's evidence against the other defendant was greater than the case against their own clients. If we'd been in better moods, their flimsy efforts would have been laughable. Thankfully, the judge denied those motions.

When the defense teams were given the opportunity to present their cases, Kyger's attorney announced that his defense rested. Confused, I leaned forward to ask the D.A. what that meant. He quietly explained that Kyger was willing to rely on a lack of evidence against him.

A Family Meal

When Judge Meyer adjourned the courtroom for lunch recess on the third day of trial, he ordered us all to reconvene ninety minutes later. My mother, my sister Debbie, her two sons, and I walked about a block to a local diner we'd tried a few days earlier. We were quickly seated in a booth along the side wall of the restaurant. Right after our waitress had taken our order, the Kyger and Hammer families walked in, playfully bantering as if they were all together in the Rutherford County Seat to celebrate a promotion or a family birthday. As a hostess seated them in the center of the restaurant, our table fell silent. Had my dad been there, I suspect our family would have either stormed out of the restaurant in defiant protest or exchanged the words that had been bottled up inside for ten months. Instead, we lowered our voices and dripped with rage as Kyger and Hammer laughed and enjoyed their families.

My nephews Jonathan and Patrick, then fourteen and sixteen, were seething. They'd spent the previous summer working in the store alongside my dad, who they adored. They'd not yet cultivated the careful social art of "managing" their feelings, and were venting by describing what they'd like to do to our fellow diners. As Debbie tried to soothe them, I could see my mother growing more visibly upset.

"Well aren't they just carrying on?" she remarked.

She didn't try to hide the bitter edge in her voice.

Then, with a resigned sigh, she added, "That really bothers me."

"Mom," I asked, feeling as if it was my duty as the de facto male head of our family, "do you want to leave? We can grab some food from another restaurant on the square."

"No," she said definitively. "They will not run us out. They've done enough already. We won't give them the satisfaction."

The rest of the meal was pretty quiet as the five of us bled with anger.

Recess

Later that afternoon, during a brief recess, I was standing at the urinal in the men's restroom nearest our courtroom when Hammer walked in. Separated by just a few feet, we each relieved ourselves as if we were complete strangers. And of course, in most ways we were. Except that I had grown to hate him and his brother-in-law like no other human beings on earth. And now he was within arm's reach. As I zipped my pants and washed my hands, I had another Josey Wales fantasy, calculating the odds of successfully drowning Hammer in a toilet bowl. Given the building's security, and a lifetime of safe sensible choices, I opted against it.

Quickly leaving the restroom, I thought of Jesus' admonition to those who thought themselves pretty righteous: "You have heard that it was said to those of old, 'You shall not murder; and whoever murders will be liable to judgment.' But I say to you that everyone who is angry with his brother will be liable to judgment; whoever insults his brother will be liable to the council; and whoever says, 'You fool!' will be liable to the hell of fire" (Matthew 5:21-22, ESV). Noticing how little resistance I'd had to the rogue thought of drowning Hammer, I silently admitted that he and I were probably more alike than I could ever admit publicly.

Although he was a murderer and a liar with a confident cocky posture, he had to be living in fear. And despite my dutiful façade of managing well, there was a scared little boy inside of me who was also capable of murder.

The following day, when a parade of fools offered alibi evidence, insisting that Rondol Hammer had been nowhere near the IGA on the night of November 14, 1986, my murderous rage against the vermin who'd shattered my family would again be tested.

CHAPTER ELEVEN

Innocent or Guilty?

Ron, September 20, 1987

Babe, remember when we went car shopping for you on that Friday evening after work? You picked me up at the shop, we stopped at Taco Bell, and then we hit a few dealerships?"

From the moment I was released on bond, more than three months after Wayne Robinson's murder, I began gently coaching my alibis. None of them, certainly not my beautiful bride Sharon, had any idea I was manipulating them.

Immediately after the crime, back in November, when memories might have been fresher, I was insisting that the police had made a mistake in questioning me and in searching our home. I'd assured Sharon it would all get cleared up. But by the time I really needed alibis, more than three months had passed. Without ever realizing they were being duped, the people who loved me, the employees who worked with me, and the other unwitting pawns in my web of self-protection were easy to manipulate. The only deception that bothered me was Sharon. She trusted me, and I abused that trust by convincing her that the story I'd spun was true.

One morning, about a week before the trial, I was desperate for meth. But because Sharon hadn't left for work yet, I couldn't get high at home. Sick to my stomach, head aching, I kissed her on the cheek and quickly fled to my car. A day earlier I'd bought insulin needles that I'd hidden under the carpet in the trunk of my car, along with the drugs. Between our home and my shop I stopped at the old railroad trestle under Old Nashville Highway. Parking my car behind some brush, desperate for a fix, I opened the car door and pivoted to rest my feet on the damp ground from the previous night's rain. My eyes darted around the car for a coffee mug or even a soda can to mix the powdered drug into a liquid form. All I could find was an old soda pop top. Like a wild animal, I bent over and scooped dirty water from a mud hole that was within arm's reach, tapped some powder in, stirred it with the tip of a "sterile" needle, and began shooting up. Within seconds of the drug being forced into my bloodstream, I was feeling what I considered to be "normal." Some days the voices in my head told me that I needed it to survive, and other days those same wily voices convinced me that I was doing fine, and it just gave me an extra edge I needed to thrive.

My loved ones weren't the only ones being played.

Between my lying, manipulating, and then shooting up for two hours beside a muddy pothole, I'd sunk lower than I ever could have imagined.

Day of Trial

The first morning of the trial was tense at home. As I helped Sharon clip on her necklace and watched her don her best earrings, I wished for the day before I'd gotten tangled up in drugs, when we might have been heading out, instead, for a date. I would have done anything to spare her the stress and disgrace of the trial, but the reality was that I needed her—not only to testify, but to enhance the appearance that I was a hard-working upstanding business owner who was a good family man, married to a wife who believed in me. Despite the humbling indignity of the trial, she did believe in my innocence. I suspect that she couldn't bear to consider the alternative, because I knew I didn't want to imagine the day when she might discover the truth.

Sharon and I rode to the courthouse in silence. When I spotted my mother and brothers in the court square, I dropped Sharon off in front of the courthouse and went to park the car.

After two and a half days of testimony for the prosecution, the judge adjourned the court for lunch recess. Before my family left to eat lunch at a local restaurant, I ducked into a private bathroom stall and pulled a baggie out from my sock. Every day I carried meth into the courtroom and would hide in the bathroom, grab a big pinch, and snort it right there. After a quick hit, feeling more confident, I joined my family and we headed out to eat. As we walked down the front steps of the courthouse, I noticed the lead attorney on my case ducking out of sight into an alley across the street. Knowing that he'd been using coke over the months we'd been preparing for the trial, and during the days we'd been in court, I knew what he was off to do.

When we returned after lunch recess, Steve's attorneys waived their right to question witnesses and my team began parading a string of witnesses who corroborated the alibi I'd fabricated. Because I'd been so methodical about laying the groundwork of deceit, I doubted any of them suspected they were telling anything other than the truth.

Sharon was the first to testify. She said that she'd left her job in Smyrna, at 4:30 p.m. on Friday, November 14. She'd driven to my shop and waited about ten minutes before we left together to go car shopping. She described how I went inside a Taco Bell to order our food, which we ate in her car as we drove to University Ford. After a brief stop at the Ford dealership, we drove to the Stones River Nissan dealership. After taking a quick drive through the lot, we kept driving to check out what was available at a Franklin Nissan dealership, about thirty minutes away. Unsuccessful, we drove back to Murfreesboro and dropped me off at my shop, where I stayed to lock up before coming home. Soon after we arrived home, around 8:00 p.m., we received the call from Steve at the police station. My attorneys also prompted her to describe how upset I was about the theft of my police scanner.

Guy Dotson, the District Attorney, did the cross-examination. He was so good that he could have made any saint come across as a sinner. He pummeled Sharon with the same question, three times in a row. "If you could mistake any one fact, and that would keep your husband from being convicted and sent to the penitentiary for life, would you?"

"Are you asking me," she retorted, "if I'm lying right now?"

Convinced, certain, she adamantly stood by her story. My attorneys had advised me not to take the stand during the trial, and I squirmed in my seat as Sharon was being made out to be the liar that I was.

Ben McElroy, a car salesman at University Ford, had been interviewed by detectives the Monday following the murder, after they'd spoken to me in my home. When detectives had shown McElroy several pictures of suspects, which had included mine, he'd not recognized any of them.

After I learned of this exchange, I visited the dealership and approached McElroy, demanding, "Don't you remember me?"

Then I convinced him that we'd looked at a black Thunderbird on the evening in question, even though Sharon and I had actually looked at it *alone* on a different day. After my visit, the well-meaning McElroy contacted detectives to revise his account. Ten months after our alleged encounter, McElroy believed he was telling the truth. Cross-examining attorneys bore down on the conflicting stories, citing company policy that McElroy should have recorded my name on his client contact list for Friday. The earnest young man could not explain why he had not. Everyone I manipulated into lying ended up bearing a portion of the shame that belonged to me.

Joe Bianchi, who'd worked for me at the time of the murder, testified that I'd confided in him that someone had stolen my hand-held police scanner. Of course, he hadn't remembered that I'd planted that idea *after* the murder. I'd told him that because I suspected another employee, I'd not reported it to the police. Joe, who'd bought half of my auto paint business when I was raising bail money to get out of prison, and who was now a fifty-fifty partner with me in the business, also had a vested interest in believing my lies. I wouldn't be around to run the shop if I was convicted.

One of the most creative defense testimonies I'd orchestrated came from George Hope, with whom I co-owned the two-seater Piper Cherokee airplane. We'd often fly together, with me behind the controls after I'd snorted meth or coke. Most of the time I was all geeked up and he'd be so drunk he couldn't hold his head up. We were so wasted that we'd get lost and have to drop down to read road signs to find our way back to the airport. George, though, trusted me, and had no idea how compromised I was.

George testified that we'd swung by K-Mart, to pick up some fix-a-flat for one of the Piper's tires that had been losing air, and while we were in the store we'd been blocked in by the red pickup. Lou described me hopping out of his car, to shift the offending pickup into neutral, so that we could bump out of the tight spot. In the days leading up to the trial I'd "reminded him" that I'd thought it had been a truck I'd worked on at the shop, but that I'd realized once I was inside, that it wasn't. He testified that we'd been able to move the stranger's truck enough to get out of the parking spot and this was the reason my fingerprints had been inside the vehicle. Because I really had helped us shimmy out of tight spot like that in Kmart, months earlier, it was easy to convince Lou that it had been the pickup truck that had been used in the crime.

Testimony concluded on the morning of Saturday, September 26, with several rebuttal witnesses. One discrepancy in testimonies involved a witness who'd known Wayne Robinson and noticed a pickup truck reeling into the IGA parking lot right behind Robinson's car when he was returning to the store from his bank run. But this witness had identified Robinson's Oldsmobile as a four-door instead of a two-door, casting doubt on the report. While that witness had unwittingly helped our defense, Sharon's story ended up hurting us.

Detective Alford testified that Kyger's call to Sharon the night of the murder, asking me to bring clean dry clothes down to the station, had—according to police records—been at seven o'clock, when she said we'd been car shopping, and not eight o'clock, as she'd testified.

Final Arguments

The prosecution's closing arguments, crafted to convict us, highlighted: the missing hour in Sharon's testimony, my finger-prints inside the getaway vehicle and on the scanner, Steve being picked up near the scene in soaked pants without a jacket, gunshot residue that was found on his hands, and the coveralls found in the area that could be traced back to him.

And in my attorney's closing arguments, he reminded the jury of the alibi testimony placing me at my place of business at 5 p.m.

Scanning the seated jurors, he looked each one in the eye and challenged them, "If you find Mr. Hammer guilty, you gotta call these people liars or dead wrong. They told the truth, and so has Mrs. Hammer."

Steve's attorney announced that his client, who was standing on his constitutional presumption of innocence, believed in the judicial system. He suggested that the gunshot residue on Steve's hands could have easily been transferred there by any of the police officers he came in contact with on November 14. With those two brief statements, he rested.

Then Judge Meyer charged the jury with their responsibil-ity, carefully explaining the difference between direct evidence and circumstantial evidence. The jury that had been seques-tered all week, transported to and from a local hotel and unable to contact their families, was released to begin deliberations at 3:45 on Saturday afternoon.

No one else in the courtroom left, because there was no telling whether it would take fifteen minutes or fifteen days for the jury to decide our fate. Whenever they finished, we wanted to be nearby. My attorneys and I were still discussing the case when, after only thirty minutes, the head of the jury returned to speak to the judge. Seeing him emerge from the jury room, the room that had been abuzz with chatter fell silent.

"Sir, we've reached a decision on one of the defendants. And we'd like additional information . . ."

My mind raced. Whose fate had been sealed? Mine or Steve's? And had the decision been "innocent" or "guilty"? It was a horrible guessing game. But when the juror returned to the jury room, like a mouse disappearing into an unknown world through a crack in the floor, we were left wondering. When he did not emerge again, everyone in the courtroom was dismissed at 9 p.m. and ordered to return at 9 the next morning.

When we drove home after court on Saturday evening, I ranted to Sharon, the way I had all week, that I was being framed for a crime I did not commit.

"I never smoked cigarettes!" I protested indignantly. "Why would my thumbprint be on any ashtray?"

Glancing quickly sideways as I drove, I could tell that, although she believed that what I said was true, she was too weary to get riled up by me that evening.

There was other testimony with which I had qualms, but I couldn't reveal to Sharon why it was inaccurate. Because I'd been in the passenger seat, the angle of the "right thumb" print they claimed was mine couldn't have been true. Also, a woman from the liquor store had testified that I'd paid her that weekend with money that "didn't feel right." And of course there was no way I could admit the real reason the testimony was unconvincing: I'd held and burned the money.

Because the drug made me particularly paranoid, I continued to insist that I was being framed by crooked cops who just wanted a conviction, even if it cost an innocent man his freedom.

Desperation

Sharon was fast asleep when I slipped out of bed at 2 a.m. early Sunday morning. I drove toward the edge of town to a hulking brown brick church with tall columns, First Baptist of Murfreesboro. I was in suicide mode once again, and was passionately bargaining with God.

Getting out of my car, I fell down to my knees on the steps of the church, bawling my eyes out.

"I'll never do drugs again . . ."

"I'll never touch alcohol . . ."

"I'll live for you . . ."

Although no one was around, I was so unglued that I really didn't care who saw me sobbing and shouting out to the heavens. For almost two hours I used any ploy I could think of to leverage my paltry offerings to strike a deal that would eliminate all consequences for what I'd done. I had but one scenario in mind for what God's magical intervention would look like: God would wield his mighty arm and all charges against me would be dropped.

On the final morning of my trial, I was actually in the same position that had led to my crime in the first place: I was trying to purchase something I wanted desperately, and didn't care what it cost.

Moment of Truth

"Jury's back! Come on, let's go!"

A bailiff had stepped outside the courthouse, into the darkness of that late-September Sunday night, to gather up those of us who'd stepped away from the courtroom for some fresh air.

Glancing at my watch, I saw that it was 9:05 p.m. My mother, sisters and baby brother had been laughing about something that had happened the previous week, but the mood quickly shifted as we rose to go inside and hear the verdict. I helped my mother up from a bench and we all returned to the courthouse in silence.

Once we were assembled, the judge called the courtroom to order and the jury filed back in, taking their familiar seats. The judge warned those gathered in the courtroom that no loud outbursts would be tolerated.

Turning to the jury foreman, an older gentleman in his mid-sixties, the judge asked, "Has the jury reached a verdict?"

"We have, your honor," he replied carefully.

"May I see the verdict?"

The foreman handed the bailiff a piece of paper that was delivered to the judge. After reading it, the judge, stone-faced, sent the paper back to the foreman.

I searched both of their faces, but neither revealed a hint of what was written.

Two deputies stepped from their posts beside the door leading to the judge's chambers and stepped to stand near our defense team.

Solemnly, the judge asked, "On the charge against Steve Mitchell Kyger, of murder in the first degree, what does the jury find?"

Hands trembling, reading the paper he'd handed to the judge, the foreman announced, "We find Steve Mitchell Kyger guilty of murder in the first degree."

Though no one spoke, the room filled with sighs of relief and despair. My sister began to sob. I turned toward Steve, who appeared both stunned and resigned.

The dance between the judge and the foreman continued as the foreman announced that Steve had also been found guilty of armed robbery and joy riding.

With every word, my mind raced to calculate the implications of each of Steve's convictions for me. Did his murder conviction mean I was less likely or more likely to be convicted? I knew the jury believed that I had driven the getaway vehicle, so if Steve had been convicted of joy riding, then I probably would as well.

Time slowed when the judge asked, "And on the charge against Rondol Lee Hammer, of murder in the first degree, what does the jury find?"

Eyes glued to the paper in his hands, the foreman read rotely, "We find Rondol Lee Hammer guilty of murder in the first degree."

Audible expressions of delight and agony again vibrated through the room.

The sounds of the foreman's voice were drowned out and I heard nothing more. Already disoriented by the drugs, and traumatized by the announcement, I stood stunned until the foreman and judge stopped speaking. The judge said words about sentencing at a later date to be determined by the court and then the sound of his gavel prompted me to turn around and say goodbye to my family. I hugged and kissed my wife and my mother, and then we were handcuffed and led out of the courtroom and into waiting patrol cars.

My new life had just begun.

CHAPTER TWELVE

Hearing God's Still Small Voice

Phillip, November 14, 1987

Having the trial behind us was a relief. The satisfaction of hearing "guilty," "guilty," "guilty," "guilty," "guilty," "guilty," on all six charges, was dampened only by the reality that even though justice had been done, it would not restore my father to our family. When Kyger's and Hammer's families had wept openly in the wake of the verdict, I suspect they were tasting the sting of loss and absence that had consumed my own family during the previous ten months. Yet they still had the opportunity to look their son, husband, or brother in the eye, embrace his warm body, feel his arms around them, and say goodbye. My mother, and our whole family, had been robbed of that opportunity. With guilty verdicts recorded in the court's records, and Kyger and Hammer at last safely behind bars for good, we awaited notice of their sentencing date. During that short season I continued to hope that they would remain incarcerated for the rest of my mother's life.

Susan was thirty-eight weeks pregnant with our third when I received a call at the store that Nathaniel had thrown up at school. Andrew was napping and she asked if I could pick up Nathaniel, who'd caught the stomach bug that had been going through the school. I had the flexibility to get him and we were just one block from home when he threw up again in our Pontiac. After I delivered him to Susan, for cleanup and a nap, I scrubbed the mess out of the car before returning to the store.

With appropriate synchronicity to the kitchen calendar displaying "Friday the Thirteenth," both Susan and nineteen-month-old Andrew were also hit with the virus. Thankfully, Woody suggested I stay home with them that day. Nathaniel was on the mend, resting in bed, and as I was rushing down the hall with a load of laundry, I glanced into the bathroom to see one of the most pitiful sights imaginable. Round-bellied Susan was on the bathroom floor, holding her hair out of her face, face stretched over the toilet, as she gently rubbed Andrew's back. Little Andrew, with a pretty cute little round belly of his own, was resting beside her, poised to vomit as well.

After Andrew did vomit—down the side of the bathroom trash can and onto the bathroom rug—I helped him back into his toddler bed. When I returned to bring Susan a glass of water, she was again vomiting violently. Setting the water on the bathroom counter, I pulled a hair band out of the drawer to pull her hair back. Sporting the worst ponytail ever, she continued to moan in agony. When she felt completely empty, and I was helping her to her feet, I heard her squeal in pain.

"I'm sorry, did I step on your foot?" I asked.

"No," she said, "I just had a shooting pain in my side."

When I helped her limp back to the bedroom, she rolled into bed exhausted.

"I'm going to get Andrew a sippy cup," I told her, "and then clean up the bathroom."

About ten or fifteen minutes later, while I was wiping down the toilet, I heard another higher pitched moan.

"You okay, Susan?" I hollered down the hall.

"Uhhh . . ." Susan hedged, as if deciding how to answer my question.

"What?" I asked. "What is it?"

With a noticeable edge of fear in her voice, Susan admitted, "I think I'm in labor."

No, I thought, not yet. Susan wasn't due until the end of the month. Dropping my rag, I rushed down the hall to our bedroom.

"Are you sure?" I asked, hoping the sharp pains she was feeling were flu-related.

Her face was pale, and I knew she hadn't slept much the previous night or eaten all day.

"I'm pretty sure," she confirmed. "Why don't I just rest and see if it passes. I've got my notebook here by the bed, so I'll just jot down the time of each contraction. Maybe they're just Braxton Hicks and will pass. No worries yet."

I hoped desperately that she was right. I gave her a kiss on the forehead, and returned to the glamorous job of bathroom cleaning.

As I wiped the damp rag along the grout between each floor tile, I couldn't help but reflect on the convergence of Friday the thirteenth catastrophes. I actually had been preparing my heart for the challenge of this weekend, but not because I anticipated playing Florence Nightingale. Saturday would be the first anniversary of my father's murder. Throughout the week, little moments had reminded me of that fateful day I wished I could forget. When Susan had brought the boys to the store to pick up a few groceries, she parked my dad's Oldsmobile, which she'd been driving, in the parking spot where he had last parked it. A few days later, when a small group crowded around a child who'd skidded off his bike in the parking lot, I could see the crowd that had gathered around my father laying lifeless on the ground. And as I reached to make a call on the store's landline, I remembered the desperation I felt when my mother told me my father had already left home to make the bank run.

I quietly prayed that Susan's contractions would pass. I didn't want our child—who would either be our third boy or our first girl—to enter the world on a day forever marked by sadness.

Susan continued to monitor the time between contractions. By eleven o'clock, contractions were coming regularly at five-minute intervals. We knew from our previous two labors that it was time to go to the hospital. We called my mother, and asked her to come stay with the boys. She also volunteered Debbie, who was living in Tennessee while her husband was overseas, so they both came to care for pitifully sick Andrew and sleeping Nathaniel. Susan and I drove in silence, she being distracted by physical pain and me consumed with emotional pain. We were about halfway to the hospital in Nashville when I watched the clock on the dashboard of our Olds 88 creep past midnight, heralding the fateful November 14.

Really, God? Is this a cruel joke?

We pulled into the parking lot of Westside Hospital at about 12:20 am. We let the nurse in the ER know that Susan's contractions were three to four minutes apart and were admitted immediately. Staff gave Susan medication for the nausea and, determining that she was dehydrated, ordered IV fluids for her dehydration. A zealous advocate for natural childbirth, Susan had refused all types of pain medication when Nathaniel and Andrew had been born. (Though I would have welcomed anything that could have quelled my emotional suffering, no one was offering me anything.)

Admitted to a labor room, Susan and I were left alone as her labor continued to progress. I would support her as she did Lamaze breathing, and wipe her forehead with a cool washcloth. At around three o'clock we noticed that her contractions had begun to slow. By my logic, this felt like a gift, as if her body knew that it needed rest. But because the medical team believed she'd passed the point of no return in her labor, in terms of preserving the baby's health, the doctor on call ordered a Pitocin drip in order to speed her labor. As the words fell from her lips, I knew how Susan would react. She viewed these medically manufactured contractions, believed to be more aggressive and painful than natural ones, with scorn. When those contractions were accompanied by a pain-relieving epidural, they were tolerable. But for the woman refusing pain medication, they could be particularly brutal.

As Susan closed her eyes to wait for the contractions to ramp back up, I brushed some hair from her face and held her hand, before falling back into the chair beside her bed. What strength, I marveled, in such a delicate container. Resting my head in my hands, I prayed. Groaning inside, I cried out to God in a Psalm-like lament.

"God, where are you? I don't understand, but I want to trust you. I can see how this is a blessing, but my heart is wounded and afraid. Help!"

A year earlier God had failed to protect my family. If God were all-powerful, then He'd allowed evil. And if he'd allowed it once, He could allow it again. Did Susan's labor setback signal impending complications? Though I'd trusted God for years, I was no longer sure God was reliable. Unsure that God was listening, uncertain if God cared, and unable to know if God would intervene, I also knew that the weight of what was before us was too much for me to carry.

"God," I finally said, feeling resigned to what would be, "this is all on you."

Above all else, I knew that the Bible revealed God as a deliverer. And that's exactly who I needed God to be for my wife, for my family, for me.

After two hours of harder-than-hoped-for labor, Susan gave birth to our first daughter, who we named Susanna Summer. My dad had been shot at 5:15 p.m. on November 14, 1986 and precious Susanna was born at 5:15 a.m. on November 14, 1987. When my father was shot, darkness was falling. And when Susanna was born in the wee morning hour, it was as if she was ushering light back into the world.

I'd spent a year wallowing in darkness. When nurses handed me my six-and-a-half-pound baby girl, swaddled in a soft clean white blanket, the gentle rhythmic promise of Scripture filled my heart and mind: "The steadfast love of the Lord never ceases; his mercies never come to an end; they are new every morning; great is your faithfulness" (Lamentations 3:22-23, ESV). By God's grace, death had been replaced with life.

As I held Susanna to my chest, I opened my heart to God, begging, "When the calendar turns to November 14 each year, I want to think of Susanna's birth before my dad's death."

That day, a prayer was answered. No one in my family could sit around in sackcloth and ashes that day, reliving the past. We had a new life to celebrate.

CHAPTER THIRTEEN

Shackled in Chains

Ron, November 21, 1987

After the verdict had been read at the trial, Steve and I had been whisked away in separate patrol cars, delivered to an adult detention center. Before we were processed, we were caged in different holding cells, containing nothing more than a drain, a shower, and a concrete slab to sit on.

Then we were put through the humiliating motions of processing. Stripped naked, we were told to hold our arms up over our heads. As it had been at the jail when I'd been held on bond, guards with big bottles of disinfectant sprayed us, turning us around and spraying again as if they were basting chickens. Then they corralled us over toward nearby showers, where we were ordered to rinse off. When we pushed a button, we had thirty seconds of water before it stopped. Then we were handed clothes and ordered to get dressed.

The routine felt oddly familiar because the inhumanity of our treatment resonated with my experience in Vietnam. At seventeen I'd forged my parents' signatures and signed on to serve my country. At the end of the war my marine unit was sent in to remote areas to rescue POWs and soldiers who were missing in action. When I was still no more than a boy, I'd witnessed my fellow soldiers treat many of the Vietnamese people like animals, burning the homes of innocent villagers, in the name of smoking out the Viet Cong, and committing unspeakable atrocities against innocent civilians. Most days, I kept my head down and did what I was commanded to do. But one day, when I saw two soldiers from my unit raping a girl who looked to be no more than twelve, something in me snapped. I went crazy and jumped on the one who was lying on top of her, beating him and pulling him off of her. When the other tried to handle me, I went berserk on him, too. I can't say exactly why I snapped, but I do know that when my father had been drinking when my sisters and brothers and I were young, he would beat us. I think that the vulnerable child in me, who couldn't defend myself, related to that helpless child. Now under lock and key I was, once again, vulnerable to the whims of authorities. For years I'd tried not to think about the horrors I'd witnessed in Vietnam, but my sympathy for the people there increased while I was in prison. The difference, of course, was that I had done something unspeakable, and worthy of punishment, and most of them had not.

After less than a week in the detention center, Steve and I were both transferred to Cockrill Bend prison, before being taken to the Turney Center Industrial Prison. Turney was like a small city being run by the inmates where prison administrators and guards exercised little control. The doors inside the prison were unlocked during the night and during the day. Violence was rampant; prisoners made and sold hooch; they trafficked drugs freely. The facility was understaffed, and had no cameras and no steel doors.

Most nights, as I drifted off to sleep, my mind would be in high gear. I'd badger God, "Why Lord? How could you have let the gun go off?" Then I'd curse myself, and turn the spotlight back onto me. "Why did you have a gun? Why were you doing this?" Every night I would dream of the crime, never sleeping peacefully. I'd see the gun go off in my dreams, and wake up screaming, "I'm sorry! I'm so sorry!" The first time it happened, Steve, who shared a cell with me at Turney, thought someone was roughing me up in our cell. But eventually he learned to just tell me to go back to sleep.

At the end of breakfast in the chow hall one morning, as we were heading out, Steve whispered, "This boy said he was gonna beat my brains out when we get to the ball field. Watch my back to make sure there ain't two of them."

I knew Steve could hold his own. He wasn't asking me to fight with him. He was only asking me to make sure it was a fair fight. If he was scared, he wasn't letting on. We went to the ball field, but he didn't see the guy who'd threatened him. When he couldn't find them, Steve and I returned to the cell we shared. We'd been friends since we were boys, and our lives were still inextricably joined.

I'd taken a run before breakfast, and was only wearing my running shoes and shorts. Steve and I were discussing how to handle the threat when we saw a pair of guys coming our way. In the front was Big Sam Brown, a power lifter who was five feet ten inches tall and 245 pounds. Behind him was Christopher Wright, who'd threatened Steve. As they approached the cell, both still holding coffee cups from breakfast, I stood with my back against the wall to let Steve and Wright fight.

When they entered the cell, Wright, who looked pretty angry, handed his coffee to Brown.

"Here," he said, turning to Brown, "hold this while I knock this bitch out."

The moment he had the mug, Brown threw both cups of burning hot coffee, with salt added for extra excruciating pain, on my bare chest. When I felt the boiling liquid burn my flesh, something snapped inside me and I lost it.

Brown never had time to hit me. Instinctively, I elbowed him and then grabbed the long ponytail that fell down his back. Yanking his head down, I kneed him in the face over and over again, wiping him through the hot slippery coffee. In my uncontrolled rage I busted his eye, broke his nose, and then dragged all 245 pounds of him down the hall by his hair. Completely unaware of what might have been happening between Steve and Wright, out of my mind, I beat on Brown a really long time as prisoners gathered around to holler and cheer. There weren't any guards around, so no one was breaking up the fight. Eventually a SWAT team came in, cuffing us both from behind, and holding our arms up behind us as far as possible to control us. We were both hauled off to the hole. Neither one of us received medical treatment, which I'd learn was normally reserved only for stabbings.

The following day guards dragged me out of the cell and brought me before a disciplinary board that met in a small room in the prison wing set aside for solitary confinement. I couldn't wear a shirt because my body was raw.

One of the members of the disciplinary action team was a woman.

When she saw me she gasped, "Oh my God! What happened?"

I'd suffered third degree burns, and my skin bubbled all the way down to my beltline. I couldn't wear a shirt for weeks and would sit in my cell and peel pieces of skin off my stomach.

Steve had taught me to never offer anything and never answer anything. It was one of the reasons I'd never been afraid that he'd give me up as the shooter before or during our trial. He'd taken his knocks in prison before and wasn't about to snitch on anyone.

All I said to her alarmed query was, "I don't know."

When the board realized they weren't going to get anything out of me, they brought in Brown.

He was in a pretty foul mess. Guards had to lead him in because, having been kneed in the face by a madman about fifty times, he couldn't see.

Word got around the prison, and no one messed with me after that. There would be plenty of other fights, but I'd done what I needed to do the first time I got jumped. I earned respect.

November 14

When the anniversary of the murder rolled around, Steve and I had still not been sentenced. On Saturday, November 14, I couldn't get Wayne Robinson out of my mind. I kept reliving the moment when the gun went off.

I called Sharon at about seven in the morning. Because it was the weekend, she'd been planning to come visit.

"Hey babe," I said, "can you send me some money?"

"What do you need money for?" she asked.

"I need to get some food from the commissary," I lied. "And I need money for stamps. I just need fifty."

My voice was getting more agitated.

"Okay," she said, recognizing my tone and withdrawing a bit, to protect herself. "Should I just bring it when I come this afternoon?"

"No," I said firmly, "I don't want you to come."

"But," she protested, "I was going to bring—"

"No!" I barked. "Today isn't a good day. I just need the money."

Hurt, Sharon quietly agreed.

When we hung up, I hated myself for the way I'd treated her. I knew she didn't deserve it. But the anniversary had hit me hard, and I was hurting inside. I couldn't erase the picture of the gun exploding between Wayne Robinson and me. Later that afternoon, with the money Sharon had wired in hand, I bought a drug called meperidine. It was a really strong pain pill used by dentists. I took it at five and it knocked me out until the next day.

Though I continued to use various drugs in prison, from the moment I heard the verdict read, I never touched any kind of meth again. It would have been easy to, because it was plentiful in prison. But it was as if meth and I had been in a heated battle, like I had with Brown, and there was no forgiveness in my heart for meth. Meth was guilty. Period.

I finally visited the prison clinic, where the psychiatrist prescribed Elavil, a psychotropic drug that robbed me of my thoughts and made me want to sleep all night and all day. I'd sleep through chow and when Sharon visited, I'd nod off during our time together. I couldn't bear to face the reality of what I'd done. As long as I can remember I've loved working and staying active. So when I could no longer show up for work, I asked the doctor to take me off of Elavil.

This put me back at square one, where I wasn't sleeping at night. I'd exhaust my body during the day, doing pushups, jumping jacks, and other exercises, all so I could sleep at night. I'd also purchase Valium that had been smuggled in by guards or visitors, from other inmates.

With anxious energy pulsing through my body, I felt particularly trapped in my cell at night. Although I wanted to run for miles and miles, I was trapped in a cell six feet wide and nine feet long. In the thin corridor between my bed and the next cell, I would pace three steps, pivot, and pace three steps back in the opposite direction. Three steps north. Pivot. Three steps south. Though not as effective as running, or immediate as drugs, the rhythm helped to calm me down when I was most agitated.

More than anything, I wanted to die. I even begged God to take my life. At night I'd accuse God, "You have nothing for me! You haven't shown me any kind of love, any kind of forgiveness. Take my life."

What I didn't realize at the time I was saying it was that giving my life to God, and really letting God take it, was exactly what I most needed.

Phillip as a senior
in high school,
voted most likely
to succeed

**Most Likely to
Succeed**

Ron at seventeen,
serving his country in
the Marine Corps

Ron and Sharon, Christmas 1985

Below:
Ron's Corvette

The last "family" photo taken with Wayne before the robbery and his murder

Left to Right:
Phillip, Delores holding Andrew, Wayne, and Nathaniel

Grocery owner shot, killed in robbery

Robinson recalled as community's friend, supporter

Two charged in IGA slaying

Brothers-in-law face charges for Robinson shooting death

'I never killed no one,' says convicted man

IGA defendants get 35 more

Jury: Kyger, Hammer guilty

Brothers-in-law convicted on all counts in IGA case

Murder in the first degree

Ron with his mom and dad during a visit in 2002

Ron running in a 1998 race while in prison

Phillip holding Susanna, "God's still small voice"

The Wayne Robinson family in 1988
Back Row: Patrick, Andrew, Phillip, Steve (Debbie's husband),
Debbie
Front Row: Jonathan, Susan, Nathaniel, Delores holding
Susanna

Phillip and Ron's first meeting after Ron's release, May 2015

Delores, Phillip, and Ron in Ron's mother's home

Ron, Phillip, and Susan Robinson

Phillip and Ron at Shenandoah Church

Sharing at New
Vision Baptist,
Redeemed for
Life conference

Pastor
Spurgeon
sharing about
Ron and Sha-
ron's wedding
cake at RFL
conference

Phillip and Ron, May 2015

CHAPTER FOURTEEN

Sentenced

Phillip, December 21, 1987

Our little Susanna was just five weeks old on the day when our family hoped to close this chapter of our lives once and for all at the sentencing hearing for Hammer and Kyger. Because Susan needed to be home with the children, she wasn't able to attend.

December 21, literally and figuratively the longest night of the year, was the kind of day that aptly marked that season of the life Susan and I shared. Awake by 4 a.m., I donned my signature uniform of a dress shirt and navy tie, with khaki pants, quietly leaving the house and arriving at my uncle's store two hours before sunrise to get things in order. I opened the safe, prepared the tills, let in the department heads, received deliveries, and prepped the store to be ready for our first customer. Work was my safe place. It's where I could hide.

After three busy hours at the store, I picked up my mother to drive together to the courthouse. Before we left, I helped her fill out paperwork for government benefits she was still due to receive. As I had on the day of the murder, the way I managed what was inside of me was by managing that which was outside of me. Problems at the store on the weekend? I'd drive right over. Mother needed a home repair? I'd be there, toolbox in hand. Susan's car not working, and needing to get the baby to the pediatrician? I was on taxi duty. Although my wife *saw* me, late evenings and intermittently on weekends, I was chronically emotionally absent from her. Unable to be fully present to myself, there was no way I could be fully present with her.

When I'd be out, at Sears or at a restaurant, acquaintances would often stop me to chat. At some point in our conversation, they'd pause and become serious, asking, "How are you managing?" And when I answered that I was managing well enough, I wasn't lying. I *was* managing well. Was I feeling my feelings? No. Was I processing my grief? No. Was I able to be fully present in conversations and relationships? No. And although I kept the plates spinning, I lived with a deep ache that I believed could be filled if someone—my wife, my friends, my church—could be fully present and responsive to me. I'd not yet discovered that I was the problem.

My mother and I arrived at the courthouse, parked in the city parking structure, and slipped into the courtroom about fifteen minutes before nine. Methodically, we marched to our usual seats the way people gravitate to a familiar pew at church. But if there was to be anything holy about this day, it would be that God's justice would be served.

Opinions

It had been three months since the trial. A few weeks after the verdict had been announced, Officer McMichael, a probation officer whose job was to make recommendations to the judge regarding sentencing, interviewed members of our family. These interviews become the official "Victims' Statements," which were read, by him, at the sentencing hearing.

When the officer described my mother's wishes, I reached over to hold her hand.

Passionless, he read, "Mrs. Robinson stated that she is not only having problems dealing with the loss of her husband, but more especially the circumstances under which he died. She described the act as 'sneaky, senseless and unnecessary.' Mrs. Robinson also referred to her husband's generous nature. According to Mrs. Robinson, approximately one month prior to his death, the victim gave $50.00 to a man who needed money to return to his home out of state. The man was a stranger to Mr. Robinson, and he knew in all probability he would not be repaid. According to Mrs. Robinson, her husband would have given money to the defendants if they'd asked."

I was pleased that the court record would reveal something of my father beyond his leading role as "victim."

The officer concluded, "It is Mrs. Robinson's opinion that both defendants should be imprisoned forever so that they will never be able to do to another family what they did to hers."

Hearing her sniff, I reached into my mother's purse and handed her a tissue.

Moving on to my statement, Officer McMichael read, "The son of the victim referred to his father's death as 'vicious and cruel.' He described his father as a 'generous man, almost to a fault,' and cannot help but feel anger at his death. Phillip stated that he felt the decision of the jury was fair and felt relief that the trial was over."

We'd made it through the agonizing trial and were now finally in the home stretch.

He continued, "He does not, however, feel that justice has been done as no amount of action taken by the criminal justice system would ever be able to compensate for the loss of his father. Although he feels some compassion for the defendants' families it is his opinion that both Steve Kyger and Rondol Hammer should spend as much time in prison as possible."

Officer McMichael also relayed the conversation he'd had with my sister. Debbie had told the officer that my father had called her to wish her a happy birthday on November 13, the day before he was killed. Now, she explained, her birthday would always be linked to his death. And her sons expressed their sorrow for the loss of relationship they might have enjoyed with their grandfather.

Even my uncle Woody and Hollis McCary, whose truck had been stolen and used as the getaway vehicle, weighed in to say that these men should be punished.

To our chagrin, family members of both men were also afforded the opportunity to speak on their behalf. Some also read letters from people "back home" who described the decency, generosity, and helpfulness of Kyger and Hammer. I felt anger swelling in my chest as witness after witness testified that these jokers were the salt of the earth. Really? Although it's possible these character witnesses believed what they were saying, Kyger and Hammer were, in my imagination, less than human.

As these far-from-impartial observers gushed about a pair of upstanding citizens who sounded nothing like the men in the courtroom, I mentally scrolled through the tall stack of job applications I'd read over the years in the store. Was Johnny's math teacher telling the truth? Or was our prospective bag boy really a monster in Converse sneakers? Did Abigail's previous boss know what she was really like, or had Abigail pulled the wool over his eyes? Suffice it to say, I would never read another recommendation letter without a great deal of skepticism.

I understood what the defense was trying to accomplish, but how could anyone in that courtroom, other than their families, take these pleas for grace seriously? They were laughable.

After listening to both the victims' statements and the defense's pleas for leniency, Judge Meyer spoke.

"I have read the pre-sentencing reports on both men," he offered, "and I find both men to be persistent and dangerous offenders."

I breathed a sigh of relief, knowing that the legal language meant they'd receive weighty sentences.

He then solemnly announced that each would receive a life sentence, the maximum sentence for first-degree murder. Then he added the maximum sentence for armed robbery, thirty-five years, and tacked on three more for the joy riding conviction. He also ordered Kyger and Hammer to pay $10,000 in restitution, should they ever have access to that sum of money.

At this point in the judge's remarks, Hammer had apparently listened to all he could take.

"I sit here and listen to everybody talking for me," he burst out. "Well, I'm gonna say something for myself!"

Those of us sitting in the courtroom were stunned by this outburst from a man we'd never heard speak at the trial. We were also a little surprised that the judge didn't stop him immediately. I waited on pins and needles for the judge to drop a heavy gavel and yell, "Order in the court!"

Hammer continued, turning to look right at my mother, "Mrs. Robinson, I am so sorry for you, but I never killed no one. I wasn't there."

I glanced at my mother's expression, and it was clear that she wasn't having it. Though she'd eyeballed Kyger and Hammer during her testimony, that had been on her terms. During his rant, she averted her eyes from his.

Tipping his face toward the judge, Hammer said in a calmer voice, "I never killed no one, your Honor."

The judge didn't seem rattled by the outburst. It was his courtroom and he remained in charge. The proceedings ended and Hammer and Kyger were escorted out by Sheriff's deputies to return to their cages.

As we descended the courthouse steps, I turned to my mom and assured her, "This is it. We did it. This is the final chapter."

I believed what I was saying was true. I just had no idea what God had in store for us.

CHAPTER FIFTEEN

Witness to Another Murder

Ron, March 8, 1988

After the sentencing, the reality of the hell I was living in gripped me in a whole new way. There was no way I would ever get out of prison, not with a life sentence *plus* thirty-eight years. While I wanted to die, the sweetness of death had, time and time again, eluded me. And I continued to be tortured, waking and sleeping, by the horrific memory of what I'd done.

Though most of my life was no longer in my control, I fought desperately to control what I could.

Handling My Business

All I really wanted to do was to mind my own business. I never went looking for trouble, but in such tight quarters, trouble found me. In those moments when it was unavoidable, the kickboxing, martial arts, and close hand combat skills I'd learned in the Marines were my best friends.

Although I wish it were otherwise, more fights followed that first one with Steve. When a couple of guys from a Muslim gang jumped me in my cell—over a bag of Raisin Bran—I lost my cool like I had with Brown. My training kicked in and as I rolled around with one of them on the floor, I stuck my thumb down into his eye socket and gouged the eye out of his head.

In another fight I bit a guy's ear off and spit it into the toilet in his cell. Spitting blood out of my mouth I taunted, "I've got Hep C! I hope you don't catch it."

You didn't have to have a physical altercation with me to know I was an angry man. Anyone who encountered me could tell I was mad at the world, mad at myself, and mad at God. When I'd get into those fights early on in my sentence, I really didn't care whether I lived or died.

I was fighting one guy, when I noticed a knife in his sock.

I challenged him, "Break your knife out! Cuz I'm gonna push it down your throat."

Whenever someone would get up in my face, I'd give it right back to them

"You got the right one," I'd bark back at them. "I'll carry you to hell with me, cuz I don't care."

I didn't. Death would have been a welcome relief.

Wanting to Stay Numb

During the daytime I kept my body and mind busy to avoid what was inside me. I lifted weights and I was running fifty to sixty miles a week. Nighttime was the most difficult. When I'd hit the mattress at night, with no distractions to occupy my mind, I'd get all choked up. I felt entirely alone and horribly ashamed. In addition to my own pain, I was carrying the pain of others: the Robinsons, my lovely wife Sharon who I adored, my parents, and everyone else who cared about me.

At night I'd wet toilet paper, roll it in a ball, and stick it in my ears in an attempt to create homemade earplugs. It was a weak attempt to try to block out a portion of the constant noise that carried into the night. And because there always seemed to be light streaming in from bright outside lights, or those on the unit, I tied a bandana over my eyes at night so I could sleep. During headcounts throughout the night, though, guards would kick the steel doors on each cell, making prisoners move to prove we weren't dummies. These bed checks, where guards were required to glean a head count of prisoners, happened at 9:15, 10 p.m., 3 a.m., and 5 a.m.

But no matter how much light and sound I tried to keep out, there was no way to avoid the pain I carried inside.

It's why I was continuing to smoke weed, take Valium, and try anything else I could get my hands on that would numb the pain.

Commotion

One evening, just after dark, I'd returned from the chow hall and was getting ready to head down the hall to the showers when I heard a commotion outside my window. The first thing I did was to turn off the light in my cell, because I assumed guys outside were looking in my cell watching me undress before my shower. But when I glanced out the window again, I could see that three men, huddled up talking to each other, had their backs turned to me. The windows had bars welded across them, and I could only open mine a few inches to hear snippets of the conversation outside. I could tell from the men's tone and the few words I gleaned that something was about to go down. They were conspiring about beating someone up.

Curiosity glued me to my bunk in the darkness of my tiny cell.

When a figure began walking down a long hall in our direction, they became silent and still. I knew that a bus had come in from Fort Pillow earlier in the evening. Fort Pillow is a West Tennessee prison more than a hundred years old, and had a reputation for working prisoners long hot grueling hours in the cotton fields.

The new inmate heading in their direction was carrying the heavy mattress he'd been issued over his head, and all of his belongings were in a single knit bag. Once he arrived in his cell, guards would take the bag from him.

But he never made it.

When he was about thirty feet from my window, the three men darted out of the shadows and attacked him. Because the weight of the mattress had forced his head down, he never saw them. I watched in stunned silence as all three men beat him mercilessly. The only sound I heard were his grunts.

Why doesn't he fight back?

When the three men released him, he dropped to the ground as they dashed away into the darkness.

I assumed they'd simply knocked him unconscious. But it made me sick to my stomach knowing he was lying there in need of help.

The thought that haunted me waking and sleeping, the image of Wayne Robinson lying helplessly on the sidewalk while I fled, flashed through my mind. Jumping into my pants, I dashed down the hall.

By the time I reached the front door, the nearest correctional officer had locked the door and was shouting for all inmates to return to their cells.

"But I think there's a guy out there who needs help!" I spouted, gasping for breath.

"I know!" he barked. "Now get to your cell!"

Knowing that if I couldn't get outside through the door I still had a front row seat to whatever would happen next, I hurried back to my cell, kept the light off, and peered out my window.

Two officers were standing by the victim of the attack.

Why aren't they bending over to help him?

One was talking on his radio and the other shined a flashlight on the prison's newest inmate. Cold chills shimmered across my body and I felt suddenly weak.

A large pool of blood had spilled out of the man, and I knew he was dead. The reason he hadn't fought back, and the reason he could make no sounds other than grunts, was because his attackers had been viciously stabbing him to death.

Falling into my bed, I was completely unnerved. I cried out to God asking him to take me from the cruel awful world in which I now lived. That night, exhausted and overwhelmed with grief, I fell asleep without either a bandana over my eyes or earplugs in my ears. When I woke up a few hours later, I became instantly aware of the familiar nighttime noises—radios, guards' voices, men talking—and lights.

Standing, I cautiously stepped toward the window and looked outside. Though the inmate's body had been removed, a huge bloodstain on the ground remained. But the blood I saw didn't belong to the unfortunate nameless inmate who'd been jumped a few hours earlier. The blood I saw belonged to Wayne Robinson.

After the gun had fired, and he'd fallen to the ground, I'd dropped to my knees as blood began to seep out of him. Though I was hopped up on liquor and meth, every part of my body wanted to help the man who never deserved to be shot.

"I'm sorry, I'm sorry!" I'd announced, while sobbing. "I'm sorry . . ."

Had he been a car, I would have known exactly what to do. But as blood began to seep from his side, soaking through his undershirt and dress shirt, dripping down his coat and onto the pavement, I froze. I had no idea how to undo what had been done. I also didn't have a free hand. My left one was clutching a bag filled with bills I'd believed would satisfy, and my right one held a pistol I was certain had been empty.

Wrong on both counts.

"Come on, let's go," Steve had barked.

In the moment I'd turned to run away with Steve, I'd chosen my life over the life of Mr. Wayne Robinson.

That choice that haunted me every day and every night is what had thrust me out of my cell that evening, as if I could ever undo what I'd done.

After that night I dipped into a deep depression for several weeks. I was even transferred to another unit because I couldn't look out that window without seeing Wayne Robinson lying on the pavement as the life drained out of him. At one level I knew he wasn't outside my window and never had been. But because the image haunted me so, I felt like I was losing my mind.

I never shared with Sharon the darkest horrors of prison. But in the weeks that followed that brutal attack, I did share my emotional problems with my mom.

"Honey," she'd coo in a soothing voice, "You got to put your faith in God's hands. You must believe in him."

Each time I hung up with her, or shuffled back to my cell after a visit with my parents, I considered what she said. But her words, ones I knew had been life-giving for her, jangled around in my head with no traction for me.

God was a million miles away from my six-foot by nine-foot cell.

Respect Earned

Word traveled quickly around the prison, and I was known as someone who was tough as nails. Anyone who did mess with me knew they were doing so at their own risk.

What no one on the inside knew—what I couldn't let them know—was that I underneath my hard exterior I was more vulnerable than they could imagine. I wasn't a hardened lifer who'd committed so many murders that he was callous. Heck, my crime had been an accidental shooting! And the same heart that would never want to see my mother suffer, the heart that longed to take care of my precious Sharon, was broken in half not just for myself, but for the wife and family of Mr. Wayne Robinson.

CHAPTER SIXTEEN

Stuck

Phillip, November 19, 1988

I never hurt no one! Mrs. Robinson, I am so sorry for you, but I never killed no one. I wasn't there!"

The words I'd heard spoken so forcefully at sentencing, and had reread in the newspaper the next day, had been engraved in my memory. My mother's, too. I'd rolled them over in my heart and mind countless times during the year, trying to make sense of them. I finally decided that they were words that, although addressed to my mother, were never meant to serve her. They were meant to serve Rondol Hammer. They were an act—for his family, for his attorneys, for the court. They were words that a guilty person would parrot in his imitation of an innocent person.

They were also words that threw a wrench into the gears of my heart, and the work that needed to happen in there. Not long after the sentencing, I'd overheard my mother telling a neighbor that she had no one to forgive, since both Kyger and Hammer denied responsibility.

"How could I forgive someone who denied any part in killing my husband?"

Her insight, if not her practice, was a valid one. How do we forgive someone, even in the privacy of our own hearts, who doesn't take responsibility for their offense?

Haunted by that saintly Father Charles Strobel, the man who'd so brazenly suggested forgiveness within hours of his mother's murder, I'd made an appointment to speak to my pastor, Mike Thomas, about feeling stuck in unforgiveness two years after the murder. I was still dubious of kneejerk forgiveness, but I knew I didn't want to feel the way I was feeling. More often than I cared to admit, my mind would wander to the day of my father's murder, and those thoughts would generate anger, blame, bitterness, and judgment. They forced me to recognize a darkness in my heart of which I wasn't proud.

"How do you forgive someone," I asked Brother Mike, my friend and pastor, sitting across from me at a local joint called Donut Country, "when they deny their guilt?"

"It's harder," he admitted. "It's definitely harder."

His words hung between us I tried to digest them.

"So what am I supposed to do?" I demanded. "I know I'm supposed to forgive, but I don't know how. It feels impossible."

I'd always known that this—forgiveness—was the story into which I'd been called as a Christian. The day after my father's murder I was badgering my pastor to let me stand in the pulpit and talk about God's forgiveness of sinners, both the heinous variety like the one who'd killed my dad and also the churchy variety like me and a lot of folks who sat in the pews of my church. God's radical forgiveness was the foundation on which I'd built my life. But somehow, imitating God's forgiveness proved more difficult than I ever could have imagined. If little Nathaniel lied to me, or if Susan spent too much money on one of the kids' birthday parties, I could forgive. But this? Forgiving Steve Kyger and Rondol Hammer felt like more than I could manage.

Brother Mike encouraged me to keep working at forgiveness. To give it time. To be gentle and patient with myself. To keep at it. And while one person might have left Donut Country with a renewed energy to forgive, I left feeling vindicated that I'd not yet forgiven these men. My dull response clearly reflected more on the condition of my heart than the wisdom of the counsel I'd received.

Delayed Homecoming

Eyeing my watch as I hustled to the parking lot, I calculated how long it would take me to get to my mother's house to pick up Nathaniel, Andrew, and Susanna. Susan had been traveling for her part-time job as a McCormick spice merchandiser, and I didn't expect her home until midnight. When I arrived at my mother's, the kids were batting balloons left over from Susanna's first birthday party that we'd celebrated that weekend. I thanked my mom, buckled the kids into their car seats, and drove home.

After an easy dinner of mac and cheese with peas and hot dogs, I gave the kids baths and tucked them into bed. Feeling pretty pooped by eight o'clock, I breathed a prayer of thanksgiving for the work Susan did every day, caring for our children. When I'd cleaned up the kitchen, I sat down and read the paper and then watched "L.A. Law" on television. Around ten, my lids became heavy and I drifted off to sleep.

When I woke, I glanced at the living room clock. It read 11:47. Although I knew I'd have trouble falling asleep again, I was glad to be able to greet Susan. I picked up the paper and continued reading, glancing occasionally at the clock. When it read midnight, I began to feel concerned. The drive from Winchester Red Food store was about ninety minutes, and I knew that if Susan had gotten a late start, she would have called to let me know. When the long hand ticked past 12:15, I began to fear the worst. Had Susan been in an accident? Had she stopped for gas and run into shady characters? Had she fallen asleep at the wheel? Anxious, my imagination began to spiral into dark places.

Neither Susan nor I had a cell phone. I considered calling the state troopers or highway patrol. Was it too soon? My mind raced for solutions. Ultimately I decided that the best thing to do was to stay home, by our phone, in case Susan called. Or worse, if a hospital or police station called. I felt as helpless as I had when my father's body had been splayed out in the IGA parking lot.

By one o'clock I was completely undone. I considered calling my mother to come be in the house with the kids so that I could get in my car and trace the route I knew Susan would travel. But if she'd gotten a flat tire, and had to exchange it for the spare in her trunk, an hour delay was still within range. If she wasn't home by two, I'd call my mother and call the police.

When I heard a car rumble up the driveway, the clock read 1:25 am. Heart racing, I jumped to my feet, and unlocked the door. Bag over her shoulder, Susan dragged herself up the front walk, onto the porch, and through the front door.

Seeing me, she began, "You didn't need to wait up—"

With more fear in my voice than I'd expected, I blurted out, "Where have you been?!"

Seeming surprised by what was, in my mind, the most logical question in the world, Susan calmly answered, "The manager allowed me to stay after closing because there were so many holiday spices and gravy displays to set up."

Her tone indicated that the matter was a simple one. My heart, though, was convinced otherwise.

Dumbfounded, I blurted, "Well, next time, please find a way to let me know you'll be late."

Susan's expression let me know my reaction was over the top. She could see I was all worked up, but she didn't necessarily know why.

Honestly, neither did I.

"Okay," she agreed, with a hint of confusion. "I'm really tired and need to go to bed now, though. Who knows what time the kids will wake up."

We both got ready for bed in silence and curled up, back to back, in the bed we shared.

Detachment

Over the next week, I was cool with Susan. I busied myself more than usual at work and maintained a safe emotional distance from her, as well. But my tendency toward self-protection waged war against my people-pleasing nature. The stalemate forced me to deal with the turmoil I felt inside. I spent lots of time, throughout the week, wrestling with God to understand the hot chaos bubbling inside me.

Friday morning, while Susan slept, I composed a letter in an attempt to unpack it, for both of us.

Dear Susan,

I expect you've noticed I've been distant this past week as I've tried to find equilibrium in my relationship with God and you. If I have seemed distant or remote, I apologize. The ground I've covered with God this past week is so personal and so profound that any attempt to express it in this note will fall short. But I want you to know what's going on with me.

I hadn't meant to exclude her from my processing, but I had such trouble understanding my reaction myself, I'd had to do some hard work with God to begin to understand it.

First, I've realized that I'm not exempt from bad things happening to the people that I love. My dad's death revealed this. Second, the only thing in this world that makes me feel vulnerable is losing you. I don't even trust God to see me through it. So when my heart gets even the slightest hint that something bad might have befallen you, I despair. I've been asking myself this week, "What is lacking in my relationship with God" and "Is my love for Susan impaired?" I've questioned the two most important relationships in my life.

If I can't trust God with my greatest fear, what use is my relationship with Him? And does my possessive passion of you even bring God glory? I don't know if I'm supposed to change or, honestly, if I want to.

The reflections were more honest than I'd usually be.

I don't know how long it will take me to work this out, but I won't let my fears lead me down the road to the thing that I fear: losing you as the love of my life.

Love, Phillip

Folding the letter, as if to protect its delicate vulnerable contents, I wrote Susan's name on the outside and carefully placed it on my pillow for her to find when she woke up with the children.

As I drove to the store in the dark, I felt naked and exposed. I could no longer hide, from my wife or from myself, the vulnerability that my father's death had exposed in me.

CHAPTER SEVENTEEN

An Act of Mercy

Ron, February 27, 1990

I was sitting on my bunk watching the Andy Griffith Show when I heard a body being slammed against the outside of my solid steel cell door. Instinctively on high alert, I slid open my cell to get a look.

Two inmates were wrestling on the ground in a large pool of blood. The man on top was Vinny Jameson. He was known in our unit for his illegal activities. The man on the bottom, fighting for his life, was Dale Brothers. Dale was a friend from my work crew who'd recently been teaching me guitar chords. Pinned on his back, blood poured from Dale's blue shirt as he struggled for his life.

For a third time I was witnessing a man dying in a pool of his own blood. But this time I reacted swiftly. And as instinctive as a "flight" response had been three years earlier, danger now triggered "fight" instead.

In a flash I was kneeling behind Vinny, locking him into a rear chokehold. Using the training I'd received in the Marine Corps a decade earlier, I choked him unconscious and removed the knife from his lifeless grip.

Shouting orders to those who'd gathered to watch, I instructed three other guys to help me lift our friend. Holding him horizontally, we carried Dale to the prison clinic. As we turned the corner to leave our unit, guards who'd been alerted to the situation rushed through a circle of prisoners to apprehend Vinny. After we set Dale down on a stretcher in the clinic, he was quickly loaded into an ambulance and rushed to a nearby hospital.

Only time would tell if he would survive.

Existing

For the previous three years in prison my *own* goal each day had been to survive.

Anyone reading my rap sheet or seeing my prison uniform would naturally assume I was like every other hardened criminal in the facility, but I never felt like I belonged. I don't mean that I didn't belong because I was innocent—though I did continue to proclaim my innocence—I just knew myself to be someone other than a lot of the guys I met in prison. They seemed, to me, to be a different *breed* from me or anyone I knew. I knew I was paying the price for the choices I'd made, the lives I'd harmed, but I never felt at home in an environment designed to contain animals.

Basically, I became a loner. I devoted myself to my job on the maintenance crew to occupy my mind.

Though my heart was beating, I wasn't living. The bright lights outside the prison at night meant that I hadn't seen stars in all the time I'd been locked up. I'd forgotten what delicious food tasted like. The lie I carried, that I'd had nothing to do with the death of Wayne Robinson, gnawed at my heart.

I couldn't see any purpose for my life.

Inevitable Meeting

Returning to my cell after delivering Dale to the infirmary, I noticed my shirt was covered in his blood. When guards allowed me to clean up, the adrenaline slowly began to drain from my body. As I scraped dried blood off my arms under the stream of lukewarm water, I began to understand the danger I'd survived and wondered if it would follow me. I never would have chosen to mess with Vinny Jameson. And now he'd be seeking revenge.

When I found out the next week that Vinny had been given three years in maximum security, I breathed a little easier. For the time being.

But about two years later, my supervisor on the maintenance crew where I worked assigned me to the prison's maximum security unit. I was expected to mop the floors, clean the showers and toilets and sinks, and empty the trash.

My first day on the job I kept my head down as I passed Vinny's cell.

He spotted me anyway.

"Hey, Hammer!" he hollered as I passed. "That's your name, right?"

Protected by the steel bars between us, I paused and turned toward Vinny. I knew I'd have to face him one day and this was that day. I expected to see venom dripping from his teeth, but his face was kinder than I'd expected.

"Man," he began, "I've wanted to thank you for what you did."

I looked behind me to see if he was talking to someone else. I was the only one in the hall.

"If you hadn't stopped me, I would have killed Brothers that day."

I knew it was true. After a touch-and-go week in ICU, Dale had barely escaped with his life.

"But if I had succeeded," he continued, as if he really had been waiting years to tell me, "I'd never have gotten out of here. And now I've only got twenty-two months left. My wife and I are back together and I'll be able to see my seven-year-old daughter."

"That's great, man," I answered, filled with relief and genuine happiness for him. "Congratulations."

Knowing I couldn't linger long without agitating the guards, I pushed my mop cart and kept moving.

When I reached the shower room and began cleaning tile walls, I kept thinking about Vinny's bright future. Though my lawyer kept appealing my verdict, I had little hope of ever being released. I'd cringed when Vinny mentioned his reunion with his wife because my relationship with Sharon was so rocky. I hoped it would weather my incarceration, but I wasn't sure. Vinny, though, was happy and had dreams for the future. He had a reason to live.

Did I?

The Letter

The unspoken dream I held in my heart was to be released while my mother and father were still living. If I was ever released, like Vinny, would *living* begin then? It was pretty hard to find a good reason to live in prison.

But as I was wrestling to find a purpose in my meaningless life, I could always remember the day I rescued Dale: *February 7, 1990*. As opposed to November 14, 1986, on this day a man's life was saved, not stolen, because of me. If one good deed could have cancelled out the bad, I would have been free that day. But I wasn't. Though I didn't yet understand God's plan for me, my gut told me what I'd later learn in the Bible: redemption can't be earned. Though the day was a meaningful one for me, it couldn't free my soul.

During his recovery, Dale—who was released from prison not long after his attack—wrote me a letter thanking me for saving his life. As I read it, tears streamed down my face.

He also included a letter that I would turn over to prison authorities to keep in my file.

It read, in part:

To whom it may concern,

On February 7, 1990, I was imprisoned at the Turney Center Industrial Prison where Mr. Rondol Hammer saved my life.

I was working as a commercial cleaner. My responsibility was to keep the restrooms and showers clean for approximately thirty to forty men and to do my best to pass all inspections. A week or two earlier, I found a plastic jug filled with homemade wine in our restroom which turned out to belong to Mr. Vinny Jameson. Mr. Jameson and myself had unkind words concerning the wine being in our area.

February 7, I found another jug of homemade wine in Unit Three's restroom and disposed of it. I told Mr. Jameson that I had poured it out. He responded angrily, and once again we exchanged unpleasant words.

Mr. Jameson left and returned a short time later, confronting me in the Unit 3 corridor, cursing me and pulling a knife from under his shirt. At that time, I panicked and started to run, but was unable to get away from him. Suddenly, I felt a burning pain and was robbed of my strength. Mr. Jameson had stabbed me in the kidney. Screaming, he continued to lunge the knife at my face and neck.

I might have died there that day.

During the attack I remember having regrets of never being able to tell my family how sorry I was for the grief I had caused them, but most of all I realized I had not made peace with God. However God sent me a crutch that day. Mr. Rondol Hammer will always hold a place in my heart for being there that day and overpowering Mr. Jameson, and somehow being able to take away a knife from such an outraged man, who was already sitting on top of me trying to take my life.

I never had a chance to thank Mr. Hammer or tell him how I felt, because after the incident I was rushed to the hospital, but I now have the pleasure of doing so. I hope to make a difference in someone's life as Mr. Hammer has in mine. I feel I am alive today because the courage Mr. Hammer put forth. He has changed my life.

Given the chance, I know Mr. Hammer would show the utmost concern for all of society. I know decisions concerning time reductions and/or release from prison must be very difficult, but I pray that you find it in your hearts to take Mr. Hammer's request very serious. He

is a man that I know does not take life for granted and he has com-
passion for his fellow man.

   Sincerely,
   Dale Brothers

Folding Dale's letter, I wiped away tears with the back of my arm. Though I had no confidence it would sway the parole board, who regularly read glowing recommendations for the worst offenders, I would submit it to the warden to be placed in my file for consideration by the board when, Lord willing, I sat before them one day.

But Dale's letter meant something even more to me. In the jungle of prison, I felt as though I'd at last been seen. Dale's words reminded me I was still human. And if Dale could see who I really was, perhaps God had not forgotten me.

Maybe my purpose wasn't just to survive. Maybe there was more for me.

CHAPTER EIGHTEEN

Faces

Phillip; November 18, 1994

People pleaser.

Active church leader.

Loving husband and father.

Productive grocery department manager.

Five years after the murder of my father, those around me saw only the impressive shine of the mask I allowed them to see. While most assumed me to be a gracious forgiving Christian man, some even admiring me for it, few noticed that I'd donned a mask of "perfection" because it was the only way I knew to keep functioning. As long as that mask did its job, I'd never have to deal with the unforgiveness that bubbled in my deep places.

Although that mask was slowly suffocating me, I couldn't imagine living without it.

Evening at the TPAC

In the spring of 1994, Susan and I were thrilled to have gotten tickets to see *Phantom of the Opera* at the Tennessee Performing Arts Center in downtown Nashville. When a friend of ours heard we'd be going, she brought her cassette tape recording of

Phantom to church for us to borrow, and also shared the sound-track to another one of her favorite musicals, *Les Miserables*. It was the only other show Susan and I had seen at the TPAC and we'd thoroughly enjoyed it.

A few weeks later, with the words already humming in our heads and hearts, we donned our "theater" clothes, oriented our babysitter, kissed the kids goodbye and drove into Nashville. It was one of only a handful of true "dates" Susan and I carved out when our children were young. We splurged by eating at an Italian restaurant in the city before the performance. Settling in our seats just as the overhead lights blinked to signal the start of the show, we were eager to enjoy the performance we'd read and heard so much about. The cast that evening did not disappoint. We'd enjoyed learning the music and lyrics to Phantom on the cassette player in our living room, and the live performance was breathtaking.

When Susan visited the restroom at intermission, I noticed a nagging in my gut. In ways I couldn't yet understand, and certainly resisted, I recognized something of myself in the Phantom. Disfigured since birth, he hid his ugliness in the shadows, donning a mask that kept others from ever seeing who he really was. While my disfigurement was not physical, the unresolved conflict in my heart toward the men who'd taken my father's life had become spiritually and emotionally crippling. Like the Phantom, I had no interest in letting others see the ugliness that had grown in my heart. Susan, who wasn't as easily fooled as those who saw me in my more public roles, was the only one privy to the real condition of my heart. While at some level the truth was as hidden from me as it was from others, she recognized what the conflict was doing to me.

I hid it, or so I thought, from my pastor. When he'd reached out to me, I mouthed the Christian words about forgiveness that I accepted intellectually, but I didn't let him see the reality: the fullness of the radically gracious and transforming power of the gospel of Christ had not yet penetrated my heart.

A Forgiven Sinner

A few weeks after we saw the show, I was feeling under the weather. I'd made it through Sunday morning worship, but felt completely beat. Susan had taken the kids to the park so I could have some down time before evening services. I'd been reading in a chair as the notes of the *Les Miserables* soundtrack filled the room. When Susan and I had seen *Les Mis* years earlier, we'd enjoyed it as much as we'd enjoyed *The Phantom*, but the depth of Victor Hugo's moving story of unlikely redemption was finding real traction in my deep places.

When a man named Jean Valjean is released from prison, after years of harsh labor for stealing a loaf of bread, he is obligated to carry papers detailing his crime and punishment. Valjean's past makes it impossible for him to thrive in the present. The parolee finds compassion, love, food and rest through a local bishop, but he repays the bishop's kindness by stealing valuable silver tableware from the parish. Hours later Valjean is stopped by the police and found to be in possession of the stolen goods known to belong to the bishop. Officers drag him, with the silver, to the bishop's home.

Having already deduced that Valjean had made away with the silver, the bishop exuberantly greets the entourage by addressing Valjean as if he's a beloved old friend: "I'm glad to see you. But I gave you the candlesticks, too, which are silver like the rest and would bring two hundred francs. Why didn't you take them along with your cutlery?"[1]

Until that moment, Valjean's experience had taught him to expect what was due him: law, judgment, punishment. Undone by the bishop's mercy, Valjean struggled to comprehend the grace that he had received.

---

[1] Victor Hugo, translated by Lee Fahnesstock and Norman MacAfee, *Les Miserables.* (New York: Signet Classics, 2013) p. 103.

FORGIVENESS IN THE FIRST DEGREE | 137

As if my illness had weakened the walls that guarded my heart, Herbert Kretzmer's moving lyrics penetrated my spirit and I fell to my knees on the living room carpet and began to sob. The soaring melodies from the 1987 Original Broadway Cast recording, especially the song describing the bishop's gift of unbridled mercy, had reached deep into my heart. In them I tasted a bit of the expansive reality of the gospel in a way I'd not known it before.

Though I knew those around me saw me wearing the mask of the bishop, I knew myself, in that moment, to be Jean Valjean. But not the free man. I was the Valjean who'd been imprisoned—inside physical walls and outside them—until he tasted, once and for all, the cleansing mercy of extravagant grace.

Could I ever experience such pure unadulterated grace? Could I be set free from my own prison?

Sinner or Saint

Heart splayed open, I rolled over on my back and continued to listen to the show.

Hugo contrasts the reputable "sinner," Valjean, to his nemesis, Javert, a police inspector consumed with law, order and punishment. Ostensibly, like me, Javert plays the "saint."

Toward the end of the musical, in the chaos of a political demonstration, Valjean has the opportunity to execute Javert. When they're alone, however, Valjean instead shows Javert the mercy he once received. Eventually Javert takes his own life because he's unable to embrace the mercy offered to him and extend it generously to others.

The same thing was killing me.

Like a soul-eating bacteria, the disease inside me that righteously clung to law over mercy, vengeance over grace, was consuming me alive.

Steve Kryger and Rondol Hammer might have been imprisoned by physical walls, but the prison I'd erected around my heart—to deny my feelings, to resist grace—had kept my spirit bound. My senses were dulled, keeping me from noticing the twinkly starry skies. Food tasted bland. Though the circumstances of my life seemed picturesque to most—the loving wife, great kids, supportive church community, satisfying work—I alone knew that my life stank as a result of the rot in my heart.

Stuck, I didn't know how much longer I could live under the weight of the mask I'd been unable to remove on my own.

Finding Freedom

Although I understood what Scripture said about forgiveness, I couldn't honestly say that I'd forgiven Steve Kyger and Rondol Hammer for killing my father. For nearly a decade I'd creatively avoided applying Scriptures about forgiving others, though it was definitely on my to-do list. I'd categorize it as one of those jobs I knew would require Herculean effort, and one at which I still might fail. Every few months I'd size up the project, acknowledge the mammoth nature of the task, and set it aside. My prayers always sounded pretty much the same, "God, I know I have to forgive these guys. I'm stuck." Then I'd conclude with some version of a prayer nicety like, "God, I know you can help me with this." This spiritual blind spot allowed me to continue feeling pretty justified in hanging on to my righteous anger.

One Saturday afternoon in May of 1994 I was mowing our front lawn, rumbling along on our riding mower past a huge maple tree beside the neighbor's fence where cows had gathered to enjoy the shade of the biggest tree in our yard. Most of the trees were over seventy years old. Because I didn't prune them, a recent windstorm had rattled a lot of branches from their limbs, and they'd littered our yard.

Climbing off the mower, I began picking up sticks and tossing them into a pile at the base of the towering maple. When I finished the yard I'd pick them up and burn them in a brush pile.

Happy to be doing mindless work, I noticed that my mind had actually wandered to the almost eight-year-old beef I had with Steve Kyger and Rondol Hammer. Before I could get too worked up, I heard God's kind voice speaking to my heart.

"Son, listen to me . . ."

The voice was gentle and kind. And as I paused to listen, God made an offer I couldn't refuse.

". . . I've got this if you'll trust me."

I wish I could say that I'd reached a plateau of spiritual maturity that caused me to embrace God's offer with a joyful heart. The reality, though, was that I was just *tired*. I was tired of carrying around the dead weight of two grown men on my back.

Tossing the last of the sticks toward the base of the tree, I was finally willing to accept God's offer.

"Okay," I conceded. "I'm done with it."

The moment really was more like tired resignation than triumphant victory.

"I forgive Hammer and Kyger."

As I climbed back up on the mower to continue cutting, I began to imagine what the implications of this forgiveness might mean.

For starters, it meant that I could no longer wish them ill.

In fact, as I mowed I opened my heart and hands and offered, "God, if they're not yet believers, may they come to know you." It was both a safe prayer and a terrifying one. Because I never expected to see either one of them as they wasted their lives away in prison, they might as well experience salvation and new life behind bars. But of course, there were eternal implications, as well.

Still working it all out with God, I told Him, "If we spend eternity arm in arm, side by side, I don't like it. But I trust you with that."

That—trusting God with what I could no longer manage—was the big win. The fact that I'd allowed bitterness and anger to linger for seven years should have signaled me, years earlier, that I wasn't managing as well as I thought I was.

When I rolled the mower into the shed and hopped off for the day, I felt freer than I had in years.

Sharing Forgiveness

I waited a few days before sharing my experience with Susan. I didn't mean to keep it from her, but I had an awareness that I wanted to savor it with God a bit longer before sharing it with others.

Thursday night we'd wrestled the kids down for bed by eight and were sitting down together in the living room to unwind.

"Dear," I began, "something happened on Saturday when I was mowing."

She looked up from the catalogue she was reading.

"Are you okay?" she asked with concern. "Did you get injured?"

What I'd experienced was just the opposite of injury. In fact, I marked that moment as the beginning of healing my wounded heart that I'd put off for way too long.

"Oh no," I quickly assured her. "Nothing like that."

She looked confused as she turned her body toward mine.

"I was praying," I explained, "and I ended up forgiving Kyger and Hammer."

I still couldn't humanize them by speaking their first names. God had more work to do on my heart.

Forgiveness wasn't something that Susan or I had wrestled with aloud until now.

"So . . ." she asked carefully, ". . . what exactly does that mean? For you, I mean?"

She understood what "forgiveness" meant, but was curious how my grass-cutting moment of conversion would change the way I lived.

"That's a good question," I mused. "And I may not know yet, for sure."

She nodded in understanding.

"I guess all I can say is that I feel more . . . free."

Susan considered my testimony and asked, "So, was it like God spoke to you or was it something you just realized you needed to do?"

Weighing her question, I answered, "Both. I admitted to God that I was outmatched, and that I was really tired from carrying unforgiveness. I just have a feeling it's affected me in ways I probably don't even realize. It wasn't a joyful moment with tambourines and trombones. More like a quiet surrender."

"Philippian," Susan said, using her pet name for me, "that's great. It's really great."

Finding Freedom

I'd been feeling pretty stuck at work. After my father's store shut down, my Uncle Woody had hired me at his Bradyville Road store, but I felt unfulfilled vocationally. I'd looked around for opportunities to own and operate my own store, but none of the possibilities had come to fruition.

After my reluctant surrender in the yard, though, the snag inside me that had been released seemed to trigger other little freedoms. Emerging from a long funk, I became a better employee at the store. Being able to trust God with this weight I'd been dragging around freed me up to be a better version of me.

Six months after my yard-chore epiphany, we celebrated Susanna's seventh birthday. We gathered as family on Monday night, joined by my mom, for dinner and birthday cake. Each year Susan catered to the celebrant, and Susanna had chosen tacos and a double chocolate cake. After dinner and cake, we retired to the living room for Susanna to open her gifts. As I watched her tear open a package from my mom containing a pair of sneakers she'd wanted, and then a long-awaited goldfish from Susan and me, I noticed that the prayer I'd prayed on the day of her birth had been answered.

From being woken up with a candle-topped pancake in the shape of a seven, to her friends singing "Happy Birthday" at Campus School, to watching her slip on her new sneakers, Susanna had been at the center of our family's life for the entire day.

None of us had forgotten the death of the grandfather Susanna had not been privileged to know, but his absence was politely staged on the periphery of the day.

Finding Myself in God's Story

One morning I was reading the gospel of Luke during my morning devotions in the living room. Though I'd read the passage countless times throughout the years, the story Jesus told about two men—a righteous one and a reputable sinner—gripped me in a new way that morning.

Jesus began, "Two men went up into the temple to pray, one a Pharisee and the other a tax collector. The Pharisee, standing by himself, prayed thus: 'God, I thank you that I am not like other men, extortioners, unjust, adulterers, or even like this tax collector. I fast twice a week; I give tithes of all that I get'" (Luke 18:10-12).

It wasn't hard to see myself in Jesus' description of the religious leader. For years I'd pridefully posited myself as someone entirely other than the monsters who'd robbed my father of his money and his life. Obviously, I was the good guy.

Jesus continued on to describe the humble sinner, "But the tax collector, standing far off, would not even lift up his eyes to heaven, but beat his breast, saying, 'God, be merciful to me, a sinner!'" (Luke 18:13).

Although Jesus didn't go into detail about this sinner's rap sheet, I knew it like the back of my hand: use of illegal drugs, joy riding, armed robbery, murder in the first degree.

So when I got to the twist in the story, the one I knew was coming but had never had personal relevance before, it gripped me in a fresh way.

"I tell you," explained Jesus, about the sinner, "this man went down to his house justified, rather than the other. For everyone who exalts himself will be humbled, but the one who humbles himself will be exalted" (Luke 18:14).

God forgave those who humbled themselves before him, not those who humbled themselves before *me*. The reason my heart had been drawn to the Phantom, and to the struggle between Jean Valjean and Inspector Javert, was because I recognized myself in them. I was the Phantom. I was Javert, in desperate need of love and grace. And yet, for too many years, my well-managed heart had allowed no room for the radical grace God was offering, and into which He was inviting me.

Because I never had known them as anyone other than "vermin," and because I never would know them, since they'd be in prison for life, the work of allowing Kyger and Hammer to be fully human, releasing my desire for revenge and wishing them well, would all have to be work that would happen in my heart.

I did not imagine that I would ever see either of these men face to face.

CHAPTER NINETEEN

Steve Didn't Do It

Ron, December 25, 1996

C ome on man, he's a good guy . . ."
My friend Barbarosa invited me to go to a church service being led by folks from a Baptist church in Nashville who'd come to lead worship on a Wednesday night. I'd visited these services led by religious do-gooders before. Most of them had no idea what our lives were like on the inside. I still felt like God had no idea what life was like on the inside, because I still believed he'd abandoned me when I most needed him to save me from the consequences of my actions.

Because I had nothing else to do, I followed Barbarosa into the prison chapel and sat beside him, arms folded in front of me. These groups could really be hit or miss, but I trusted Barbarosa. When the preacher stood up in front to greet us, I thought he seemed real. Not too religious. A good guy, like Barbarosa had promised. My body softened, and I relaxed. I think I sensed that I didn't need the steely exterior that normally protected me inside the walls and could just relax.

God's Spirit filled the church that night. I recognized it in the faces and voices and hearts of the volunteers and also in the preacher's message. He talked about God's patience with people in Noah's day, and how God granted them 120 years of life during which they could turn to him! He said that God also shows great patience with us today, giving us enough time to quit living our own way and start living His way. It's up to us, as it was with folks in Noah's day, not to let time run out before giving ourselves to him.

After the message, the preacher invited forward those who wanted to give their lives completely to God. I wanted to go to the altar, but kept resisting. I noticed a tugging inside, pulling me in both directions. A voice inviting me to embrace a whole new life was niggling me to stand from my seat, walk to the front, and kneel at the altar. Another more cynical, quiet voice chided, "You've already done this, trusted God when you were a boy, and God hasn't done anything for you." This tug of war raged inside, but the strong pull of the Spirit won. On October 7, 1996, I dropped to my knees in a prison chapel and I gave my life to God. For the first time, I claimed sole responsibility for my actions as I asked the Savior into my life.

I know it sounds cliché to say that everything changed that night. In some ways, though, it did. I felt a huge burden lifted from me. I didn't' need to hide anymore. I stopped blaming God for everything, and learned to begin to look inside my own heart. When I did, I could see how self-centered I'd been. I'd still been dabbling in drugs, smoking a blunt or doing meperidine, but I never touched another drug after that night.

The next morning I was waiting at the gate to the ball field when it opened at 7 a.m. I ran three miles around the prison's quarter-mile track. Within two weeks I was running five miles every day. I am a naturally energetic person, but it was almost like there was this release of energy that had been bound up in all my sin that was released out there on the track. I loved having the time to think, away from the prison noise, drama, and chaos. It became my special time with God, who I was now seeking with my whole heart. It gave me time to repent, to offer God those areas of my life I'd never confessed or released, and to remember who I really was. Those miles on the track were a chance for me to be myself, the person God had created me to be, once again. Although I wasn't real excited about others joining me for a run, I always said yes because I knew they wouldn't be able to keep up. (I was never disappointed by this decision.) Daily, I was growing closer to God.

My Running Prayer

Every morning I sensed God's presence with me as I ran. But the Robinson family also became a part of my runs. I prayed for Wayne's wife, that she'd be taken care of the way I hoped my own mother would be taken care of. I prayed for his son, that he'd be a good husband and father to his children. I prayed for Wayne's daughter and her family. I asked God to fill the gap that had been left by the death of their father and grandfather.

I also began sharing with everyone how loving my Father was. Guys on the unit could see that I'd changed. When I'd walk past their cells on the way to a church service, they'd call out at me.

"What you going to church for, Hammerhead? You got your girl down there? You gonna score?"

Fueled by something real, I ignored their mocking.

During that season, God began to expose the shadowy areas of my heart. One of those was the chamber where I harbored unforgiveness. I started to notice the grudges I held against guys who'd borrow tuna or a six-pack of cold drinks and not return them. Or against guys when I'd overhear them make a mean comment. Or when I knew they'd gone into someone's cell and taken advantage of another sexually. I started to notice the ways I hardened my heart and held that offense against them.

I was trying to live by God's Golden Rule, doing to others what I'd want them to do to me. I was trying to live a life like Jesus lived, and this was where the rubber hit the road. During my morning runs, God was showing me these places of unforgiveness He wanted me to release to him.

So I tried. I didn't announce to any of my fellow prisoners that I forgave them—which would have felt particularly awkward and self-righteous in the cases where their offenses were against others, and not me—but I asked for God's help to assume a gracious posture toward them. I tried to treat them as if I'd forgiven them.

Trying to give forgiveness kept me busy. And it may have even distracted me from a more insidious failure in my life: I couldn't forgive myself for what I'd done. In fact, there was only one other person on earth, at that time, who knew what I'd done: Steve Kyger. And the truth was eating me up.

Knowing My Victim

During this season of spiritual awakening, when I felt God's Spirit alive inside me, I began to be more curious about the man whose life I'd taken. I wanted to learn everything I could about this man. I remembered from the trial that he had a wife, a son, and a daughter. And that each of his children had two sons.

Something inside me kept telling me I had to know this family. Whenever I'd meet a guy inside whose last name was Robinson, I'd ask if he was any relation to the Frank Robinson family. (I knew him as "Frank" because of "Frank's IGA," which had been the name of his father's store, not realizing that although his first name was Frank, his family called him Wayne.) I hunted around the prison, trying to find someone who was from Murfreesboro. I'd lived there just six years before I went to prison, but I knew that someone who'd grown up there would most likely know of the Robinson family.

I was obsessed with him. I wanted to know if Mr. Robinson was a family man. I wanted to know if he was abusive, as my father had been. What about his son? Was he a good guy? I wanted to know what kind of father his son Phillip was. I wanted to know about his boys.

As I discovered what kind of man Frank Wayne Robinson had been, a generous hardworking family man, I began to carry his memory around in my heart. I'd be brushing my teeth and would look up and see his face in the mirror. Or I'd imagine him watching over me as I worked in the prison factory, and would purpose to do the best job that I could do. I didn't know if this was coming from God, or from my subconscious, but Frank Wayne Robinson became an ever-present figure in my life.

In a way, he'd already been a presence over the last ten years. I was still waking up in the middle of the night from nightmares about the murder, shouting, "I'm sorry, I'm sorry!" (I'd lost several cellmates over it.) Or when guards would shine their bright flashlights in my face during late-night bed checks, I'd wake in a sweat that soaked my sheets. Or some joker would stomp on a milk carton, creating a loud *boom!* And each time, I'd hear the crack of the gun exploding on November 14, 1986. I'd often get depressed after instances like this one. Though no one had diagnosed it, I was suffering from all the symptoms of PTSD. I may have experienced the ripple effects of horrors I'd witnessed in Vietnam when I was younger, but I had quelled those with drugs. I never sought help to deal with those memories or to deal with the lingering trauma of taking a man's life. I didn't seek help because I didn't believe I deserved it.

If I was honest, I also didn't believe I deserved God's forgiveness.

Coming Clean

"Mom," I said in a hushed voice, "I've got to tell you something . . ."

Being in my mother's presence, being able to touch her hands, were the moments when I felt most human. She had driven down to Tennessee from her home in Virginia on Christmas day to visit me. Until then, she'd usually visited with my dad or one of my brothers or sister. This was the first time she'd visited alone. We sat across from each other, surrounded by lots of other families, in a crowded visitation room. She looked as happy to see me as if she'd been visiting me in my own living room.

Sensing the serious tone of my voice, she stopped smiling.

"What is it, Ronnie?" she asked, with concern.

"Mom . . ." I began, before getting choked up.

She pulled a folded tissue out of her purse and handed it to me.

"It's okay, honey," she cooed, "take your time."

I sucked in several deep breaths to regain my composure. After a period of silence, I spoke slowly and carefully.

"Mom, I done it," I announced.

As I spoke the words, I felt lighter than I had in years.

"Done what, Ronnie?" she asked, with concern in her eyes.

I'd offered my confession as if the weighty lie that had been squeezing the life out of me for a decade was also the first thought on everyone else's minds. Disappointed I had to say it again, I drew another breath and tried again.

"I killed Wayne Robinson. Steve didn't do it."

Her eyes widened as she processed what I'd said. Although I'd continued to deny any involvement with the murder, she had probably figured out that I'd gotten tangled up in it somehow. She knew her son-in-law Steve had had a bumpy past, and that we'd made bad choices before. Before she could respond, I started rattling my tearful apology.

"I'm so sorry I didn't tell you sooner," I said, as my whole body quivered. "I couldn't. I didn't think the gun was loaded, and I never thought it would fire. I haven't told Sharon, and I don't think I can. I'm so ashamed. I'm so sorry, mom."

She squeezed my hands as if to let me know I could stop. It was over. I could let it go.

"Honey," she said thoughtfully, "I knew something had been eating at you a long time."

Her compassion made me sob even harder. She had no interest in judging me, the son whom she loved more than her own life. She simply reflected how she'd seen this secret affecting me and hurting me. Soon we were both crying. As hard as it had been, it felt so good for someone besides Steve to know the truth.

Because my case was still under appeal, because I still loved my wife, I had no plans to tell anyone else.

Three Words

Unfortunately, my night terrors continued. Afterwards, I'd lie in bed nervously for hours asking God for forgiveness.

One morning, after another night of reliving my crime, I was praying to God when I heard a quiet voice whisper three words to my heart.

"Confess your sins."

I had no idea what that meant, because I'd been confessing my sins to God ever since I got saved. Hardheaded and hardhearted, it took me about a month to discern what that still small voice was saying to me.

God wanted me to confess to the family of Frank Wayne Robinson.

CHAPTER TWENTY

The Hand of My Father

Phillip, December 29, 1999

D on't go into the grocery business."
     "You can do better."
  "You can do anything you set your mind to."
  Two decades earlier, the voices of my college professors had scrolled through my head when I decided to leave the Colgate Darden Graduate School of Business Administration at the University of Virginia to return home to Murfreesboro.

  When I'd headed to UVA, I knew my father was disappointed I wasn't following in his footsteps by staying in town to join his business. Robinsons had been providing food to Rutherford County since my great-grandfather Wiley Robinson opened his store in the late 1890s. If I left the grocery business to pursue another kind, that legacy would die with me.

  So when I returned to the store in 1980 he was thrilled. I was kneeling in the aisle stocking ten-pound bags of Martha White self-rising flour when my dad came over with a big smile on his face. He proposed changing my title from "clerk" to "Assistant Manager," and even gave me a raise. Joining the business felt like the right thing for me and my family at that time. It's what I felt I'd been made for.

  I'd spent a lifetime learning the business from my dad. After his death, and the closing of his store, I continued in the grocery business working with my Uncle Woody at his store on Brad-yville Road, as we both continued to look for opportunities for me to own my own store. Over a decade after my father died, we identified a location on Church Street and even found a lender willing to help us build and open it.

While independent grocery stores were hurting across the country, I believed that our good name, earned by caring for customers in our community, would buoy our business.

It was an optimistic prediction.

Moving Forward

For years I'd watched my mom taking flowers to the cemetery to spend time near my father's grave. And while I'd always felt like that was her thing, and not mine, I felt drawn to go visit the cemetery during the season that we were preparing to open the new store on Church Street. I'd always wanted to own and run my own store, but in some ways, I did feel like I was doing what I was doing for my father and his memory. I was contin-uing the legacy that had begun with my grandfather, who was known to the community as "Mister Frank" and was beloved by all.

Stepping out of my car near my father's plot, I walked through the deep grass to his marker. I noticed a bouquet of daisies, no doubt from my mother's previous visit, wilted in a bronze vase. Grateful no one else was around, I let my dad know what was on my mind.

Dad, I wish we could have this conversation face to face. I really hope this is the right thing to do, and I wish I could talk to you about it. I feel like you're with me in this, and I just want to do my best. I think what God wants me to do is to allow my work to be worship of Him, and to show the world what a successful godly businessman looks like. If I can do that, I'll be happy.

My heart longed to receive my father's blessing.

Susan and I were both actively involved in New Vision Church at that time, and Al Feria, a retired preacher who also worshiped there, had become my spiritual mentor. He and his wife, Dawn, became like grandparents to our kids, inviting them to play in the pool at their apartment complex. The morning before the store opened, Al joined me as I gathered all of the employees for a short service of prayer and anointing. In my father's absence, God had provided Al to join me in shepherding that holy moment.

The grocery store had always been about family for the Robinsons. And just as I'd grown up helping my dad, all three of my children had been involved in the life of the store as they were growing up. When Andrew and Susanna were young, they set up a lemonade stand on the front sidewalk of the store, creating their own retail opportunity. Susanna, who was ten when I opened the Church Street store, still says she learned how to work hard by watching me work. When she came in, she'd do a little bit of stocking. Andrew did some stocking, as well as facing shelves, lining up all of the available stock near the front of the shelves.

But of the three, Nathaniel had been the one who'd most enjoyed working at the store. He'd worked a lot in the Church Street store during his high school years. Though he was attending the Webb school, a private high school in Bell Buckle, our store was the place where the bus picked up day students from Murfreeesboro. Before and after school, Webb kids would come into the store to get snacks and drinks.

Not long after we'd opened, we began to hear rumors from the salesmen who came through the store that a Food Lion grocery store was coming to the neighborhood. When the newspaper published that the county planning commission had approved the site, the writing was on the wall. Just as we were seeing our very best sales, the week of July Fourth, 1998, the Food Lion was being built across the street.

When other Americans face the threat of disaster—a looming hurricane or snowstorm—they brace themselves by going to the grocery store. They stock up on water and other staples they'll need as they hunker down to weather the storm. But when we became aware of the impending threat, the hungry Food Lion that would eat us for breakfast, there was absolutely nothing we could do to prepare for impact.

When the Food Lion opened up across a side street we shared, in the fall of 1998, the volume of our sales quickly dropped by half.

Margins in the grocery business were already slim, and we had none to spare. Unable to afford department managers, I worked day and night trying to manage our small store. We worked out a fragile deal with our lender that continued to let us limp along, but when a Kroger chain grocery store opened up at the beginning of 1999, and we dipped below our minimum volume for several weeks in a row, I knew we could no longer stay afloat.

Nathaniel described the closing of the store in an essay he wrote for school, which read, in part, "Often, one does not notice something until it is gone. Such is the way it was in my family's grocery store after the last gallon of milk crossed the scanner with a computerized beep. The compressors keeping everything cool were silenced. The swishing of the automatic doors was heard no more. The final noise of the lock echoed across the sparse shelves for the last time. And then there was an utter, eerie quiet. A dream had been broken with that last noise and only silent desolation remained."

His words captured, for me, the deep sadness of that day. After the last customers had been ushered out of the store, I held an employee meeting. One of those employees was my nephew Patrick, who had adored helping my father at the store as a boy, and had worked as my store's Assistant Manager. He was also part of that next generation who didn't get an opportunity at the grocery business. The number of employees was much smaller than at the meeting that had kicked off the store opening two years earlier. For those who hadn't been there at the beginning, I spoke about the optimism we'd had at our launch.

I reminded them, "We're quick to talk about God being good when his plans are matching up with ours. But I want you to hear that when they don't go the way we want, He is still good."

I let them know how much I appreciated them being a part of the store's mission. Then Al, my mentor and makeshift father figure, prayed over the staff and over me. As he spoke, I breathed a deep sigh of gratitude to God for loving me through this godly man.

New Provision

With our household budget on life support, I didn't know how we'd pay the tuition for Nathaniel's senior year of high school. I was visiting with an old high school friend in Knoxville during that season, and caught him up on all that had been happening in the life of my family.

As we were saying our goodbyes near my car, door already ajar, my friend surprised me by saying, "Phillip, I don't feel like I was a very good friend to you when your dad was killed. I'd like to cover Nathaniel's school expenses for his senior year. How much is that?"

In the absence of my earthly father, I continued to see signs that a good heavenly Father was providing for my family.

A few weeks after the store closed, I returned to dad's grave to debrief with him.

Hey dad, remember what my senior class voted that I would achieve in the school yearbook? Most likely to succeed. Well, that hasn't happened. The store is closing. It's a different world, dad! I guess I'd hoped it was still like Murfreesboro was in the sixties and seventies. I gave it a shot and I do feel like I got to show the community what it looks like to close a business well. I've tried to take care of our people the way you would have.

I think my dad would have been proud that I'd given the store my best effort.

During that period when I was missing my own dad, my heavenly Father ushered me from retail into His own business: the work of ministry. Active in the life of New Vision Church, I served on the search committee that was looking for a position that was an odd combination of skills and gifts. Our congregation needed a pastor for adult education and outreach who would also be involved with children's ministry.

Our senior pastor visited one of our committee meetings in the spring of 1999, and joined our discussion about the challenges of finding someone to wear both of these important hats.

Offering the possibility that the job might be reorganized, he suggested, "I think we can split this up."

As soon as that idea was on the table, it was like a lightbulb went off in my head. Adult education meant "Sunday School," and outreach meant coordination of visitation. I could do those.

I felt my heart start racing in my chest as I imagined the possibility of stepping into the role of pastor for adult education and outreach. Holding the idea in my heart, sharing it with Susan and praying for a few days, I scheduled an appointment to meet with my pastor.

As we met in his office, I explained, "The store's closing. Do you think this position might have my name on it?"

Mulling over my suggestion, my pastor mused, "Yeah, I could see you doing that."

Since I was on the search committee, I hardly felt like I could nominate myself! As I stepped down, my pastor offered my name and, graciously, the committee agreed to hire me. When I came on church staff working for New Vision thirty hours a week, I was still working thirty hours part-time at my uncle's store. It was one of the hardest seasons of my life! I'd get to the store at five or six in the morning, and then leave at noon to head to New Vision. It was like I had my feet in two different boats and those boats were drifting further and further apart. When Woody's store closed in December, I jumped ship and landed squarely in the world of ministry, where the church was now willing to pay me to work fulltime.

The transition from doing the work of my earthly father to doing the work of my heavenly one was a life-giving change for me. I felt God's blessing as I continued to feed the ones He loved. And as I continued to grow into God's unfolding plan for me, God continued to transform my heart.

CHAPTER TWENTY-ONE

Free at Last

Ron, February 25, 2007

Baby, there's something I've been wanting to tell you . . ." I choked out, fighting back tears.

It was Christmas of 2006, and Sharon had brought a picnic lunch to eat together. The prison allowed unopened food packages, so she'd brought fruit, chips, a loaf of bread, a pack of ham, and other sandwich fixings.

Sharon could see the concern in my face. She knew immediately that something was very wrong. For months I'd wanted to confess to her that I'd killed Wayne Robinson, but hadn't been able to gather my nerve. I knew that once I said it, everything would change.

"What is it, honey?" she asked with concern.

"Uh . . . I . . ." I stammered, unable to get the words out.

I took a deep breath and willed myself to fight back emotion.

For a decade, the only person I'd ever trusted with the truth about my role in the murder of Frank Wayne Robinson was my mother, when she'd visited me in the Christmas of 1997. I'd been very clear at that time that I was confiding in her, but that I didn't want anyone else to know. I certainly didn't want the court to find out, because my appeal was still in process. For all I knew they would want to add years to my sentence if the truth came out. I didn't want my siblings to know the truth. I didn't want my father to know. I certainly didn't want Sharon to know. But the Spirit had been nudging my heart to tell my wife the truth.

"I . . ." I tried again. "I done it."

It was out. I'd said, it.

Her face flushing with concern, she clarified, "You did what?"

I felt ill. All the years I'd insisted that the prosecution had fabricated evidence, and that I was innocent, Sharon had trusted me.

Taking a deep breath, I announced, "You're looking at the man who killed Wayne Robinson."

I quickly continued, "It was an accident. I didn't think there were any bullets in that gun. It shouldn't have fired. It should never have happened. I'm so sorry. I'm so ashamed."

Sharon sat in stunned silence as I rambled on.

Finally, I collapsed into tears.

"I'm so sorry," I repeated again and again. "I never meant to hurt you."

Sharon didn't reach over to touch me. She didn't speak.

"I . . ." she fumbled for words, "I . . . don't know what to say . . ."

Looking up, I assured her, "You don't have to say anything. This is on me."

We sat in awkward silence, neither one knowing what to say.

Looking at her watch, Sharon suddenly announced, "I think I have to go."

"Alright," I replied, feeling confused and disappointed. I feared she was so disgusted by me that she couldn't even stay in my presence.

When I glanced at her face, Sharon looked like she was in shock. I understood it was a lot to process. Stunned, gathering up her jacket and purse, Sharon stood up and left abruptly. She even left all the food she'd brought for us to share behind, despite knowing I couldn't take it to my cell and that it would be confiscated.

There was no way to calculate how much I'd hurt my bride, both in that moment and over the years. The only measure I had, which was probably a pretty accurate barometer, was that when she left that day, Sharon stopped visiting me.

The End of My Marriage

A few days after she got home, Sharon wrote me a letter telling me she wanted a divorce. I couldn't blame her. My confession had made Sharon rethink the previous two decades of our relationship and all the ways I'd harmed our marriage by continuing to lie. I don't think I'll ever know the extent to which my denial corroded our relationship. Seeing Sharon's face when I told her the truth, seeing her disappointment and hurt, was soul crushing.

For ten years, my mother had gently held the truth of what I'd done. And although the Christmas of 1997 had been my mother's first solo visit to see me, she continued to make the occasional visit by herself. During those precious times we could speak freely about what I'd shared with her.

During one of those visits, she gently challenged me.

"Honey," she suggested, "maybe you should tell Mrs. Robinson that you're sorry and that you didn't mean to do it."

The suggestion terrified me. Not only had I insisted, to Mrs. Robinson's face, that I hadn't had anything to do with her husband's death, I'd not only been involved, I'd pulled the trigger. Before my mom left that day, we prayed together, and she asked God to help me.

As she was driving home, one of my dad's favorite sayings filled my mind, "You made the bed, now you gotta lie in it."

I had made the bed. But I didn't want to lie in it.

Nudged to Action

After my mother had suggested confessing to Mrs. Robinson, I put it out of my mind. I did consider it again a few years later, but then decided it was a selfish thing to do. Why would I intentionally open up the Robinsons' wounds with a confession meant to lift a burden off of me?

But early in 2007 I'd been walking with God for ten years, and I was still suffering every day for what I had done. After one of my nightmares, I woke up in the middle of the night in a sweat and my sheets were drenched. Desperate, I dropped beside my bed to my knees and prayed to God for help.

"Why do I still live in so much pain?" I begged. "I have confessed my love for you and I accept responsibility for my sins. Why do I not feel your forgiveness?"

As I wept, I heard a quiet voice whisper to my heart.

You have not asked forgiveness from Mrs. Robinson. You have not even told her the truth about what took place.

The voice, kind and gentle, sounded something like my mom's. But I recognized it as God's gentle prompting. For twenty-one years I'd let Steve take the blame for what I'd done, and I suddenly understood that that was wrong. I'd justified my silence by reasoning that we'd committed the crime together, we'd been tried together. And now I'd seen firsthand the devastation the truth could cause. It had rained pain down on Sharon, and I didn't want to do the same thing to Wayne Robinson's widow.

But even though Sharon's reaction hadn't been what I would have hoped, and even though I was devastated losing her, I did feel a weight lifted off of me once I'd told the truth. And although the outcome was disappointing, I still knew I'd done the right thing.

At last.

In the days after I told Sharon, as I was still grieving the death of our marriage, I became convinced that I needed to contact Mrs. Robinson to take full responsibility for what had happened. While the gun firing was technically an accident, I had no interest in shifting blame for what I'd done. I should never have been there in the first place, and I wasn't going to minimize what had happened by calling it an accident. I'd gone there to do wrong, and I'd done it.

I was so determined that even my ongoing legal appeal wasn't going to stop me. I was going to tell Mrs. Robinson the truth, even if it meant I never got out of prison.

Finding Mrs. Robinson

At that time, I knew that there was a guy in the prison by the name of Boggs who was from Murfreesboro. I sent word with a guy I'd met in the library for Boggs to meet me at the chow hall. He looked confused when he met me at lunchtime.

"Would you be willing to call your mother and ask her for the address of Mrs. Robinson?" I asked.

He'd been living in Murfreesboro in 1986 and he already knew what I was in for.

Boggs looked dubious, so I started offering him incentives.

"I'll give you a book of stamps . . . no, a couple books of stamps," I threw out. "I'll pay for your phone call."

He still looked unconvinced, so I decided to up the ante.

"I'll reimburse you five-fold! Whatever it takes. I've got something that needs to be done."

I think Boggs must have thought that I meant them harm, because he tried to distance himself from my plan.

"It's really none of my business," he hedged, reluctantly. Then, hoping to send me in a new direction, he offered, "Don't you still have family in Murfreesboro?"

That, of course, was a painful subject for me. Sharon had stood by me faithfully for twenty years, but she'd had enough. Of course, I didn't blame her. Although I still loved her desperately, I let her go. What else could I do? Also, she'd moved back to Virginia years ago.

"No, I don't."

I think he was trying to keep clean, to get out of there without any infractions. I understood that. But God had placed this hard on my heart, and I had to write that letter.

Composing the Letter of My Life

There was a small desk in my cell that measured twenty-three inches by thirty inches. Even without Mrs. Robinson's address, I knew the letter had to be written. Carefully laying out a page of clean lined notebook paper in front of me, I began to write the words I'd rehearsed countless times in my head.

"Dear Mrs. Robinson . . ."

As I wrote, tears fell down my cheeks. I used the sleeve of my shirt to wipe them away before they could hit the desk. By the third page, though, the letter was stained with stubborn slippery tears. Crumpling up the pages, tossing them in the trash, I began again. I didn't need the first letter for reference, because I'd rehearsed the words so many times in my mind, that I knew them by heart before they were even penned on the page.

"Dear Mrs. Robinson," I began again.

I continued to wipe my tears with my sleeve, but they refused to slow. I made it through the fourth page before I had to abort the mission again.

Before I could produce a legible draft, I'd had to rewrite the letter five times.

Fifth Time

I knew that the letter would open wounds within the family, but I still felt it was the right thing to do. As I wrote, I prayed that God would ease the Robinsons' pain as they read my confession. Even after more than twenty years, it crushed me to relive that day. I couldn't imagine what it would be like for them.

The fifth time was a charm. I carefully aligned the stack of five pages, and folded them into thirds. Slipping them into an envelope, I carefully licked the seal and pressed it shut. I wrote my name, my prisoner number 118414, and the prison address in the upper left corner of the envelope. Then I carefully adhered two stamps in the top right corner, for good measure.

A few days later I finally persuaded Boggs to help me. I carefully wrote Mrs. Robinson's name and address in the center of the envelope: Mrs. Frank Robinson, 948 Main Street, Murfreesboro, TN 37130.

Little did I know at the time, I'd used the wrong name, since Mr. Robinson's father had gone by "Frank" and everyone knew the man I'd killed as "Wayne." I'd also been accidentally given the wrong address. And I even used the wrong zip code.

When I dropped the letter into the mail, I never expected to receive a response from anyone in the Robinson family.

Unwittingly, I'd almost guaranteed it.

CHAPTER TWENTY-TWO

The Hand of God Intervenes

Phillip, March 3, 2007

Christine Davis had lived next door to my parents for over fifty years. She'd worshiped in the same pews as them for thirty-three years. When the news reporter had interviewed her after my father's murder, she'd described him as "faithful to his church, to his family and to the community."

On Friday March 2, 2007, a letter addressed to "Mrs. Frank Robinson" landed in Christine's mailbox. While Christine had hand-delivered plenty of misplaced letters to my parents over the years, this was the first one marked in red ink, "The Department of Corrections." The ominous stamped words warned, "NECX has not inspected nor censored and is not responsible for the contents."

The name on the return address was "Rondol Hammer."

Like the rest of the town, Christine knew exactly who'd written the letter. Though twenty years had passed since the trial, she knew the name and seeing it in her mailbox enraged her. Christine's first impulse was to drop the letter right into her kitchen trashcan. But she ultimately chose to take what she considered to be a more "hand of God" approach. Christine placed the letter near the edge of her kitchen counter with the trashcan butted up against the cabinet. Over the next several days, if the letter were to fall into the trashcan, Christine decided—by a sudden gust of kitchen wind, or an accidental brushing—then the hand of God would have put it in the trashcan. Delores would be forever spared the pain of its contents and, in Christine's mind, good would have prevailed over evil.

After the weekend, as the envelope clung to the countertop, it became clear to Christine that God's will was not the local landfill. And to her credit, she kept her bargain with the Almighty. Late Monday afternoon Christine phoned my mom.

A Misplaced Letter

"Delores, this is Christine," she began hesitantly.

"Hi Christine," my mother replied, with her signature pep, "what can I do for you?"

"Well," Christine balked, suddenly unsure if she'd made the right decision. She continued, "I received a letter Friday, addressed to you, that you may not even want to read . . ."

Now curious, my mother waited for Christine to continue.

With a hint of disgust in her voice, Christine offered, "It's from the state prison. Return address says 'Rondol Hammer.'"

My mother gasped. She *did* want to read it. For years she'd been receiving reports and checking in on the public records about how Steve Kyger and Rondol Hammer were faring in prison. If one of them got into a fight, and was sent to solitary confinement, she knew it. If they kept their noses out of trouble, she knew it.

Not trusting Christine to rush next door fast enough, she chimed, "I'll be right over!"

Christine met my mother at the door and invited her into the kitchen. Sitting down, with Christine waiting patiently beside her for a report, my mother devoured the letter.

Although Christine was ready to dish, the first thing my mother did was to hurry home and pick up the phone she'd held the day I called her from the store to tell her someone had been shot. But she wasn't calling me at the grocery store. I was in my office at the church when my mother called to tell me she'd received the most surprising letter from one Rondol Hammer.

Unexpected Words

As I sat behind my desk, I listened in disbelief. Never had I imagined that either criminal would communicate with us. As my mother read me the letter, I was weighing Hammer's sincerity with every word.

Dear Mrs. Robinson,

I pray this letter finds you feeling well and in good spirits. So many times over the years I have wanted to write this letter, but always feeling too ashamed to do so, always believing that it would re-open an excess of grief in your heart. But now I truly feel that the Lord has directed me to do so.

Oh boy, I thought. Was this one of those jailhouse conversions I'd heard guys have as they approach parole? I was torn. I'd prayed for Kyger and Hammer to come to know the Lord, but I don't know that I ever really expected it to happen. My antennae were up to discern whether or not this letter was some carefully calculated ruse.

Mrs. Robinson, on the evening of November 14, 1986, I was the one that so cowardly took your husband Frank Robinson's life.

What?! Could this be true? Was this dupe trying to cover for Kyger? What were they trying to pull, anyway? I'd always imagined that Hammer had been a hapless pawn in Kyger's game. For two decades I'd harbored a particular resentment for Kyger, who I'd assumed had been the mastermind behind the crime and had pulled the trigger. If this were true, discovering that the gun that killed my father had rested in another man's hand suddenly turned my internal world upside down. It changed the story we'd lived with for two decades.

Please believe me that it truly was an accident. I never would have hurt anyone for any amount of money. As you know, several witnesses stated that Mr. Robinson and myself struggled which was true.

As I reached down to take the bag from Mr. Robinson's hand he grabbed for the pistol. Even to this day so many years later, I can't understand why the gun went off. I've wished over a million times and still wish that it would have taken my drug infested miserable life even as I write this letter. I feel so sick and weak for the terrible and unjust thing I have done. I was so terrified when the gun went off. I didn't know what to do. I know now I should have stayed there with your husband at that very moment. I died with him for as the sun will never shine in his life again nor will it in mine.

Until that moment, I'd never known exactly what had happened in that parking lot. Witnesses with conflicting stories had testified to the best of their abilities, but there had never been a clear picture of what had happened. I'd always known that there had been three people who knew for certain, but one of those was dead. If Hammer was telling the truth, I could now see that fateful exchange more clearly. I winced as I imagined my father struggling to fend off the sudden threat—not just to his life, but perhaps more immediately to the store that provided a livelihood for his family and for his employees.

I will never be able to apologize enough to you and your family for taking such a wonderful and loving man's life. I know in my heart that Frank Robinson was not just a plain simple man, but a great man loved by many and the gift to this world straight from heaven, and in me he or his name will never die. I will always tell anyone in prison or society what an amazing man Frank Robinson was and of all the wonderful ways he helped so many. Knowing what I know of him now if I would have only asked, he would've helped me get my life straight.

Over the years I'd wondered whether my dad's killer had any awareness of the impact of what he'd done. Had he—once Kyger and now Hammer—any idea of who was lost in that rash act? What I knew of those two clowns I'd read in the papers, heard rumored in the grocery store aisles, and seen in the courtroom. Because they remained mostly silent during the trial, I'd only heard their voices laughing with their families over lunch or during Hammer's outburst when he spoke right to my mother denying any involvement in the crime. The thought of both Kyger and Hammer made my skin crawl. I'd spent ten years considering them less than human, and ten more years willing to allow for their humanity and releasing it into God's hands. Although I hated to admit it, this guy now actually seemed like he might be sincere. Was he?

Mrs. Robinson, I would like for you to know what led me to such a cowardly act as to rob and steal from your husband. Society thinks that this new drug epidemic of meth has just recently surfaced. But in all reality it has been around for many years because I was hooked on this terrible drug for over two years when I committed this horrendous crime against your husband and family.

Every dime I would get would be spent to purchase this drug. I had got so bad that I didn't want to get out of bed unless I had meth to give me energy. I was working unaccountable hours every week just to support my habit.

This admission was easy to believe. And although I wanted to disbelieve him, Hammer's vulnerability was both compelling and disarming.

Myself and my former brother-in-law had never planned to rob Mr. Robinson. I was told that day while purchasing meth that all I had to do was to go there and show this man a pistol and he would give me the money. I was so weak minded and greedy that your husband paid for my lowlife act with his life. This I live with every day of my life. Many times a day I think of Frank Robinson and many times a day I ask God to please forgive me. I kneel before our Lord Jesus Christ each and every day in this tiny cell seeking forgiveness. I cannot quit thinking about Mr. Robinson. You and his family are constantly on my mind throughout everything I do. I feel that's the way it should be for when one takes another's life, he or she should live with it all the days of their life.

I pray for you and your family to forgive me and that Mr. Robinson rests in peace. I feel that he is there in spirit watching over his loved ones.

He kneels before our Lord Jesus Christ every day seeking forgiveness? He prays for our family? He thinks of my father daily? The shock and disorientation I'd felt when my mother began reading, as I first saw that awful pistol in Hammer's hands for the first time, gave way to another kind of disbelief. Had God answered my halfhearted prayers for this man who I barely considered to be human? I carefully entertained a timid willingness to believe God had.

I've always tried to do right since I've been here for I feel that he somehow is looking down on me, and knowing he was a religious man, he would want me to better my life. I have liver disease so I am sure my life will be cut short, but I want to do what your husband would have me to do if he were here directing me through this life.

In the years when Kyger and Hammer were first locked away, I would have welcomed the thought of a shortened lifespan for either of them. Although I was still glad they were behind bars, I noticed that my onetime death wish for both had waned.

I have lost everything that I have ever loved except my mother and father, and I feel in my heart I will never be with them again. I will never hold my head high for any reason. I will forever live in shame and I am sorry for all the lies I told after the crime. I just felt so lost, alone, and degraded. I was so desperate to hide my disgrace. Terrified, all I could do was keep trying to deceive anyone that would listen. Again, please forgive me.

I'm no longer involved in any drugs, but try to reform myself by living right, doing good and not evil. Taking your husband's life was evil enough to shame me for my life.

I had always wondered if either man had felt guilt, shame, or remorse for their actions. If the letter my mother was reading to me was sincere, Hammer had.

Mrs. Robinson, as I continue to pray daily for your forgiveness, I understand that it is not likely, because I ask myself if someone took my mother or father's life could I forgive them? I guess only God knows the answer but I ask you sincerely from the bottom of my heart to please try to forgive me. I will suffer all the days of my life for taking such a precious man's life. Please forgive me for the enormous pain I have caused you and your family. I am so sorry for what I have done to Mr. Robinson, you, his children, and loved ones.

May God bless you all.

I remain Sincere,

Rondol L. Hammer

My head and heart were overwhelmed with so many feelings that I struggled to make sense of what I'd heard.

"Mom," I asked, "What do you think about this?" From her uncharacteristic silence, I could tell she felt as stunned as I did. We'd vilified Kyger as the gunman in our hearts and minds for years. Discovering that we didn't know what we thought we knew felt unsettling.

"How could he have listened to the prosecution get it all wrong, without speaking up? And then be convicted?" my mom wondered aloud.

"I guess their defense depended on them denying everything," I mused, "so pointing the finger at Hammer wouldn't have served either of them."

Although we had little sympathy for either man, we couldn't ignore the difficulty of what we'd just learned. After we hung up, my mind raced. While I felt some satisfaction about hearing the truth from one of the culprits, it forced me to reconstruct what had taken place twenty-one years earlier. Like my dad trying to wrestle the gun away from his assailant, I was mentally trying to wrestle the gun from Kyger's hand and place it into Hammer's. Because the new answers we received opened up a host of new questions, I didn't really know how to think or respond. In a rare moment of emotional clarity, I did know how I *felt*: anger.

Less than an hour later I drove to my mother's house to see the letter for myself and to make a copy she could send to Debbie, who was living in Alabama. And as she handed me the pages that might just as easily have landed in the "undeliverable" box at the city post office or at the city dump if our neighbor had had her way, I wondered what they would mean for us.

My mom had spoken to Debbie earlier in the afternoon, and she reported that Debbie had been just as flabbergasted as we both were. Then she told me what Debbie had said after hearing the letter.

"Debbie said, 'I'll bet Phil will write to tell him he's forgiven.'"

I heard an edge of wariness and a smidge of disapproval. I was uncertain whose emotions that reflected—my mom's or Debbie's.

Over a decade had passed since God had set me free from the grudge I'd carried for years against Kyger and Hammer. In that time, writing a letter of forgiveness had never seriously crossed my mind.

CHAPTER TWENTY-THREE

Why I Finally Forgave Myself

Ron, March 18, 2007

When I saw the creaky mail cart wheeling my way I was pacing in my cell—three steps forward, pivot, three steps back; three steps forward, pivot, three steps back. Because I'd received a letter from my mother that week, I didn't expect the inmate assigned to postal duty to stop in front of my cell. There was a day when the best thing I could have hoped for in life was a loving supportive letter from Sharon, but I knew those days were over. I continued to pace.

"O.G.!" the young man yelled as he approached my cell. Many of the younger inmates, especially those in gangs, called me O.G.—original gangster—as a sign of respect.

Curious, I extended my hand to receive the correspondence. In the top left corner, the sender had penned the address of a church in Murfreesboro. A church? I couldn't think of anyone who'd be writing me from a church. And most of the folks I'd known in Murfreesboro had stopped communicating long ago.

Carefully tearing open the envelope, I pulled out a neatly folded piece of ivory stationery. My gaze fell to the bottom of the page.

"Phillip Robinson."

Phillip Robinson?!

I felt my heart rate increase. I knew Phillip Robinson was the son of Wayne Robinson. Assuming he'd read my letter to his mother, I suspected he might be furious. I braced myself, emotionally, for whatever anger and vitriol he might want to rain down on me.

Dear Rondol,

Mother and I received your letter. It was unexpected. I thank you for your courage in taking the time to sit down and write, thinking of others instead of yourself.

I began weeping. I never dreamed I'd hear from Wayne Robinson's son, and I certainly couldn't have imagined that when I did I'd receive kindness. I had to put the letter down, because I could no longer see clearly. Taking some deep breaths, I picked it up again.

As a Christ follower, I'm forgiven and I forgive you. That took some time, though. And God has certainly worked in my life to make that possible. There have been many changes in my life and I want you to know that you are forgiven.

Salty tears fell on the sacred page I held in my hand. For a decade I'd pored over God's word, lapping up the good news that I was forgiven by God. But in that holy moment, God's grace and forgiveness penetrated my deep places in a way I'd never imagined possible. I did not realize the weight of the burden I'd been carrying until a hand greater than my own lifted it from my shoulders. It was as if God had used the heart and pen of Phillip Robinson to release what I'd not been able to let go of on my own.

Blinded again, I sucked in air and cleared my head enough to keep reading. I stretched out my arms to hold the letter further from my face, keeping my tears from smearing it.

I hope you continue to walk with Christ as you have mentioned in your letter. I hope that the burden you carry does not interfere with your walk with Christ.

Sincerely,

Phillip Robinson

For years, the cowardly act I'd committed had eaten at me every day, torturing me mentally and spiritually. And while I understood that Jesus had sacrificed his life so that, through repentance, I could be forgiven, I had been crushed with sorrow. I'd made up my mind to live for the Lord, reading my Bible and attending church regularly. I was no longer deceiving, lying, conniving. I'd stopped using all drugs. But there was always a grey cloud following me, threatening to storm at any moment. Anything could trigger those unpredictable storms. Terror could shoot through me when I'd see the sudden burst of light from a guard's flashlight. I'd jump if I heard an unexpected explosive noise, even the backfiring of a supply truck in the factory. And I continued to wake up in a hot sweat after dreaming about the gun exploding in my hand in the parking lot of the IGA. Day and night, almost anything could trigger my deep shame and guilt.

The comfort I experienced as I read that letter was a feeling I'd never known before.

I was lighter.

I was freer.

I felt alive for the first time in twenty-one years. I finally understood, in my deep places, what it meant to be born again. Everything I'd been begging God for, for all those years, had been delivered through Phillip's letter.

Before quieting myself for sleep, I carefully put the letter back into its envelope and set it under my pillow. When I was finally able to sleep, I had joy in my heart that night.

And when I woke up in the morning, reaching under my pillow to make sure my memory hadn't fooled me, I was comforted by the thin envelope. As I rose to get ready for the day, I realized that, for the first night in years, I hadn't dreamed about Wayne Robinson.

A Brand-New Day

Before I left my cell for breakfast and work, I folded the envelope in half and carefully slid it into the back pocket of my
prison jeans. Then, during our morning break, I slipped into a
bathroom stall, pulled the letter out of my pocket, and read it
again. I carried it with me everyplace I went—chow hall, factory, library, chapel—reading it as often as I could. Grace was
being seared on my heart through Phillip Robinson's redemp-
tive words.

I forgive you.
You're forgiven.

Certain that all good gifts come from God, I praised Him for
what he'd done in Phillip's heart and what He was doing in
mine.

Suspicious

At that time, Steve and I were in the same prison. I didn't share
the letter with him right away because I wanted to savor the
sweetness of my newfound joy with the Lord. But one day, after
we'd finished lunch at the factory where we worked, I let Steve
know I'd received a letter from the Robinson family.

"I'd like for you to read the letter," I suggested.

Steve ordered, "Read it to me."

"I'd like you to read it," I repeated.

Grudgingly, he took the letter from me and read it. I
watched his face, searching for the kinds of emotional expression I'd felt when I first read it. Instead, I saw a furrowed brow
and clenched jaw.

When he finished, Steve was silent.

"Isn't that something?" I asked him.

He looked dubious.

"I just don't know, Ronnie . . ." he hedged.

Steve knew that I loved the Lord, and had been trying to
follow him the best I could. I could tell from his face that he

thought I'd been duped—first by religion, when I'd been saved ten years earlier, and now by Phillip Robinson.

"Steve," I explained enthusiastically, "He forgave me! I feel like I been dragging around Wayne Robinson's dead body for years, and I'm finally free."

"That's good for you," Steve offered, in a patronizing voice. "But I'm just not sure about this."

Steve stood up abruptly and left. Maybe, I reasoned, he needed time to process it.

Up to No Good

The next morning, Steve slid his breakfast tray beside mine and sat down. Both of our plates had a yellow mush that approximated powdered eggs, and a stale piece of toast.

"I've been dwelling on this," he said, forcefully.

His announcement confirmed my hunch. I knew the letter had affected him.

"I slept on this," he explained, "and I think he's up to something."

What?! How could he think that? But even as the question welled up in my heart, I knew the answer. Steve had been incarcerated too long, had been forced to have his guard up for too long. And now he genuinely believed that Phillip Robinson wanted trouble with me. Although I understood where Steve's reaction was coming from, I knew he was off base.

"What can he be up to, Steve?" I asked indignantly.

Prepared with an answer, Steve barked, "He's trying to get something out of you. He forgave you too easily."

Nothing about that letter caused me to believe that Phillip Robinson was the kind of conniving man, seeking his advantage over another, that Steve and I had been.

"Well," I answered, "I don't think it was easy. If it was easy, he would have done it twenty years ago."

Steve considered my reply, but I could see he wasn't buying it.

He explained, "There's something hidden beneath that letter that you're not seeing."

Steve and I both knew that lots of prisoners approaching parole suddenly "found God." They'd tell the most convincing stories to the parole board—confessing their crimes, feigning contrition, and acting like saints—because they knew that's what it took to be released. If they denied responsibility for the crime for which they'd been convicted, if they seemed cold and unrepentant, or they'd exhibited bad behavior in prison, the parole board would keep them behind bars. I could understand why those guys would make up a story to serve their own ends, but I failed to see what Phillip Robinson could gain by manipulating me.

"Steve," I protested, "I really don't think he's up to anything . . ."

Then Steve exploded, revealing what was keeping him stuck.

He burst out, "Who in the hell is gonna forgive someone who killed their dad?!"

There it was.

Those who've spent time behind bars know what it does to your soul. Those who want to survive don't risk trusting anyone. They stay on their toes and keep their guard up. If they falter, if they drop their guard for a moment, they can be taken advantage of. That necessary hardness can cause a part of them—the part that's able to recognize hope and light and goodness—to die.

Steve simply couldn't fathom the possibility of authentic heartfelt forgiveness after what we'd done. I hadn't dared to imagine it either. But when it arrived on my doorstep, the way the stork might drop off a swaddled newborn in a lunch pail, I recognized the forgiveness Phillip had extended as the very commodity in which God dealt. The breezy dove that was God's Holy Spirit *had* personally delivered new life to me!

Though Steve was dubious, I knew that this was the business God was in. And I believed that the same grace I'd received was available to Steve and to anyone else who was willing to receive it.

Sharing My Good News

Phillip's letter became so worn in the first weeks after I received it that I knew I wanted to find some way to preserve it. I also wanted to share it with my mother and father. My dad had been diagnosed with cancer, and I wanted him to have some good news. And although I could have rewritten it verbatim, I wanted them both to see the actual letter Phillip had sent me. Four weeks after I received Phillip's letter, I mailed it to my mother and asked her to put it in a very special place in her home, to save it for me. She was as amazed and delighted as I'd been. When we spoke on the phone, she said she heard life in my voice again.

My mother had been waiting twenty years for me to be set free. For the previous decade she'd seen the changes in me that others had noticed, as the Lord had worked in my life. But she could also see how wracked I'd been with shame and guilt for what I'd done. Now, whether or not I'd be released from prison during her lifetime, she knew I was free.

I did, too.

Because since the day I received Phillip's letter, waking or sleeping, I've never seen the gun go off again.

CHAPTER TWENTY-FOUR

My Buddy in Mountain City

Phillip, November 14, 2010

H ow's your buddy in Mountain City doing?"
That's how my mother would inquire about the letters
I'd been exchanging with Ron Hammer, incarcerated in a facility in Mountain City, since he'd first written her. She had been
decidedly guarded about his intentions.

But as time passed, a change in my mother's language signaled the shift that was taking place in her heart. During the
trial, and for years after, she'd referred to the defendants as
Hammer and Kyger. But as I began to get to know Ron a bit
more, and as I shared with her a bit about our exchanges, she
began to refer to him as "Mr. Hammer." As he gradually became
humanized in her imagination, she started to call him "Ron," as
I'd begun to do.

She also chose to forgive him. Though she didn't write a letter, as I had, she'd found freedom in her heart by forgiving Ron.

One morning my mom was walking with her buddies at the
mall, and their conversation turned to the subject of Mr. Rondol Hammer. It had been hard for a number of our family members and friends to understand how and why we'd chosen to
forgive. Many felt the need to express their dismay.

Mr. Harris, a gentleman about my mother's age, was growing visibly upset as she mentioned that I'd been corresponding

with Ron. He'd gone to school with my dad, and had loved him dearly.

Finally Mr. Harris exploded, "He should have been strung up at the courthouse!"

Mrs. Harris, looking embarrassed, read my mother's face. Seeing that my mother didn't agree with his sentiment, she apologized for her husband's outburst.

"We just love you, darlin'," she cooed to my mom, as her husband fumed.

My mother was gracious. She was familiar with those who shared the opinion she once did.

"Well," she sighed with resignation, "What's the option? Not forgiving eats your guts out."

I knew firsthand that she was right. My mother and I weren't some saintly altruistic heroes for whom forgiveness came easy. We were just regular people who'd been battered by bitterness. For years I'd memorized Scriptures on forgiveness, and read books on forgiveness, and felt guilty for not bursting with the kind of forgiveness I'd received from God. But God had been patient with me and continued to prompt my heart to forgive.

It actually wasn't until I received one particular letter from Ron that I understood what it was God was doing among us. It arrived at my church office about a year after we'd begun corresponding.

"Phillip," he wrote, "I'll never forget how miserable my life was even though I sought love and forgiveness from God. I lived in so much agony and despair until I received your letter that day telling me that through Christ you had forgiven me for taking your father's life. Though I was saved in 1996, I truly never knew God's sincere love and forgiveness until you shared it with me. I told my mom that Jesus put so much of His spirit in between the pages of your letter last year."

For reasons beyond my own explanation, Ron's words sank deep into my heart.

It wasn't that God's forgiveness of Ron had been insufficient. It was that God *chooses* to use people, ordinary ones like
me and like my mom, to minister his own forgiveness to others.
It was never the backup plan. It was God's big plan. In Jesus,
God had used a man with human flesh to extend His own forgiveness, and God still does the same thing through highly unlikely characters. As God had massaged our hearts over the
years—Ron's, and mine, and my mother's—we finally became
willing to submit to His good design.

So, at one level, we understood those who were baffled by
our choice to forgive. There was a day when, critical of Charles
Strobel's immediate willingness to forgive his mother's killer,
we shared their concerns and objections. But after having tried
both ways, living with a hurting hardened heart and living with
one that no longer had to carry such a heavy burden, I was
grateful for God's beautiful redemption.

Another Surprise

About two years after we'd begun our correspondence, I
grabbed a stack of papers from my mail slot at church to find a
letter with Ron's familiar handwriting on the plain white envelope. After doing a few errands around the building, I sat behind my desk and opened the letter.

Dear Phillip,

*I pray this letter finds you and your family healthy and in good
spirits. I struggle as I write this letter, asking God to help me to put
my words in the proper perspective.*

I felt my heart rate quicken. What was he about to reveal?
Whatever could he be struggling with that could be more difficult than what he'd already shared with us?

*Phillip, I'll get straight to the point, because regardless of what I
say, I feel no one will ever know the true compassion I harbor for you
and your family.*

*When I arrived and took your dad's life, I took everything from
you and your family. That I can never return and I will be eternally*

sorry for, but that night I also took money from him and his family. Phillip, I have managed to save $5000 and I wish to send it to you. I wish I could send more.

Please accept this in good faith to do with what you think your dad would want. He was a great man, helping so many so often, and Phil, I thank God for allowing you through Christ to forgive me and thank you. I remain

Sincerely,

Ron Hammer

I was shocked. Years earlier I'd read that prisoners in Tennessee could make one dollar per hour when they worked at factory jobs. I'd assumed that those who weren't blowing their money on drugs would use that money for incidentals like sodas and cigarettes. I never imagined we'd see Ron's half of the money the court had ordered Ron and Steve Kyger to pay.

I chose not to mention the promise to my mother, in case Ron, who I did believe meant well, was unable to deliver.

A Good Gift

A few days later my mother received a handwritten letter from Virginia. The return address said it was from someone named Delores Hammer. She'd remembered Ron's mother from the trial, who she'd envied for still being able to hug and speak to her son when my widowed mother hadn't had any opportunity to say goodbye to her husband. As a mother, she'd always wondered whether Ron's mother had believed him to be innocent or whether she knew, in her heart, that he'd been involved in her husband's death.

When she opened the envelope and pulled out the note from Mrs. Hammer, my mother found a cashier's check inside.

The note from Delores Hammer read:

Dear Mrs. Robinson,

I write this letter saying I'm sorry for what happened. It was a bad thing my son will live with it the rest of his life. I've always tried to teach what the right thing to do is and tried to do the best I could.

My mother's heart went out to her. She understood that most parents do the best they can and grown children will make their own choices. But Mrs. Hammer's condolences, that acknowledged the truth that had been twisted and hidden for too long, touched her heart.

Mrs. Hammer continued,

We've got so much to be thankful for. Ron has been saving this up so I am mailing it to you for him.

Love,

Delores Hammer, mother of Rondol Hammer

The check was made out in the amount of $5000.

The moment she read it, my mother called me at the church to tell me.

"What do we do with it?" she asked. The money had been stolen from the store, but the store was long gone. And my Uncle Woody, my dad's business partner, had died in 2003. Wanting to be faithful stewards of the treasure, I called Bill Whitesell, the current District Attorney who'd prosecuted the case twenty-three years earlier.

His advice? *Spend it.*

While a Hawaiian vacation was tempting, my mom's retirement nest egg was almost exhausted. So the money Ron had earned, and his mother had passed along, was a blessing to my mother.

New Life ... Again

By the beginning of 2010, our children Andrew and Susanna were both married and were both expecting their first children. Andrew and his wife Amanda welcomed their daughter, Sophia Jane, in early October. Susanna's and Josiah's child was due November 1.

As is the case with many firstborns, November 1 came and went while Susanna's baby remained happily nestled inside her. Because she'd chosen to deliver at home, with the assistance of a midwife, there wasn't quite as much pressure to deliver "on time." So we waited patiently, trusting that God was in control of when our second grandchild arrived.

Susan and I were getting ready for church on the second Sunday of the month when we both received a text message from Josiah, "We are in labor." It was about 7:30 in the morning. Because Susanna was delivering at home in a one-bedroom apartment, we knew that we were to arrive after the birth, not during. Knowing how long labors could take, Susan and I agreed to go to church and cover our responsibilities in worship and in Sunday School before heading toward Susanna's home in Franklin, which was about thirty minutes from the church.

But at 9:15, Josiah texted, "We're pushing."

Pushing meant the baby could arrive any moment! Quickly assigning our duties to others who could step in for us, we dashed out of church and headed for Franklin. (Though I did forget to find a sub for a baptism I was scheduled to perform during the second service!) Dutiful to our instructions, we sat in the parking lot of their apartment building and waited for more news about the birth, praying as we waited.

When we were still praying in my car at 2:30, I approached their apartment and gently knocked on the door. One of the two midwives opened the door, looking a big haggard. She reported that Susanna was doing an amazing job, but that it would likely be another hour or so.

Susan and I dashed out to grab a bite to eat, and continued to discuss Susanna's labor. When a woman starts pushing, it's because the baby is on its way down the birth canal. More than five hours of pushing was a very long time to be exerting that kind of stressful physical labor. The fear in my heart, which I dared not speak, was that, depending on the outcome of Susanna's labor, November 14 would now mark either two tragedies or two new lives. As we bowed our heads to pray before our meal, we continued praying, "God, protect this little child and our child Susanna. Give the midwives all they need. Em-

power Josiah with all the strength and grace he needs to em-
body You during this hour." Releasing the situation to God, I
was able to trust once again in his sovereignty.

After eating, we returned to our parking lot vigil. As the sun
began to set, I received a call from Josiah. Lilly Emmaline had
been born at 4:37 p.m. and he and Susanna were ready for her
grandparents to come in and meet her. With deep sighs of relief, we joined the new little family and met sweet Lilly.

Though she'd tarried and arrived two weeks "late," Lilly was
born on her mother's twenty-third birthday. That she also arrived on the twenty-fourth anniversary of her great-grandfather's murder was yet another confirmation that the One who
is love and life was equally alert and present to our suffering
and present to our joy.

CHAPTER TWENTY-FIVE

Will They See I'm Different?

Ron, September 3, 2014

I'd been anticipating this day for twenty-seven years.

The Tennessee Board of Parole was going to hear my case and decide whether I'd been rehabilitated. If they decided I was no longer a threat to society, had served my time with integrity, had been productive during my imprisonment, and had not committed more crimes while incarcerated, I could be eligible for release. Of course I had committed crimes while incarcerated, mostly while defending myself when provoked, but it had been years since I'd had an infraction. I'd been informed that the parole member would review my case, disciplinary record, education, work ethic, and programs I'd participated in behind bars. He'd also listen to statements from my victim's family and those who could speak on my behalf.

When I got out of bed at daybreak I'd been awake all night, too anxious to sleep. Before rising, I'd read Paul's exhortation to the church in Corinth, "'My grace is sufficient for you, for my power is made perfect in weakness.' Therefore I will boast all the more gladly of my weaknesses, so that the power of Christ may rest upon me" (2 Corinthians 12:9, ESV). I begged God to give me enough grace to see me through the day. And the Robinsons, too. I hated that their wounds would be ripped open once again on my account.

Too nervous to eat, I stayed in my cell during breakfast. At 8:30 a.m. I was called to go to the parole hearing room for the 9:30 meeting. On the long walk to the designated building, I felt weak. I continued to pray, asking God for strength.

When I stepped into a waiting room in Northeast Correctional Facility, I saw seventeen family members who'd come to support me and speak on my behalf. While it felt good to see them and know the love they had for me, I felt no joy—only humility and shame.

As much as I pined for freedom, the heaviest concern on my heart wasn't whether I'd be released ahead of schedule. The thought that always danced in and out of my consciousness was whether or not I could communicate to the Robinson family that I wasn't the same man I'd been in 1986. While the opinion that mattered the most at the hearing was that of the parole officer, who represented the board, the ones that mattered most to me were those of Phillip and his mother. I'd spent weeks massaging sentences in my mind, seeking words that would best communicate my remorse and also the transformation God had done in my life.

I was wearing a pair of cheap prison-issue blue jeans, made for women, with a large stripe down the side that read TENNESSEE DEPARTMENT OF CORRECTIONS. My light blue shirt had the same words emblazoned on the back. I also wore sneakers with my prisoner number written in permanent marker inside the tongue. For almost three decades I'd been reduced to a number: 118414. It's what I put on every piece of mail I wrote, and I knew it was how the state of Tennessee identified me. There wasn't a day I forgot it. No one in my life—not the prison officials, not the guards, not the other prisoners—knew me as a person with passions and fears, family and friends, hopes and dreams. For 9,845 days, I had been reduced to being 118414. I prayed that the Parole Board, and the Robinsons, would be able to see the man I'd become.

Ten people could be admitted into the meeting room where the hearing would be held. Among them were my mother, my sister Kathy, my great-nephew Ryan, his mother, and my pastor, Carter.

The notable absence that day was my father. When I'd spoken to him on the phone in November of 2008, his doctors believed he'd beaten cancer and was on his way to a full recovery. During our call he said that his only dream was to see me come home before he died. He said it's what had helped him get through his cancer. Before we hung up, he promised to come visit me the following week. The next day, he died. When Phillip learned of it, he wrote me the most beautiful sympathy card after my dad's death. He reminded me that although November 14 reminds him of a tragic event, God had transformed that day by the birth of his daughter, Susanna. He encouraged me by saying that God could also redeem my own dad's death. Oddly, as I witnessed the degree of grace this man extended to me, I understood why Steve, and other guys on my unit, were convinced that Phillip had a sinister motive for communicating with me. They had no way of knowing that this was a very special man who allowed God to live through him.

If my father was a painful absence in that faithful group of cheerleaders, the notable presence was my former wife, Sharon. We'd started communicating about a year before I went up for parole, and she'd made a few visits to see me. We both believed that God brought us back together. And now, the day that we never thought would come had finally arrived.

Although it was hard to imagine what life would be like on the outside—living in a world of laptop computers, and cell phones, and social media—there had been one dream in my heart that had never waned during my imprisonment. It wasn't so different from my dad's dream of seeing me released before he died. In it, I saw myself sitting in church and holding my mother's hand like I did when I was a little boy. I could think of nothing better, and I understood that realizing that dream was dependent on my performance at the hearing.

So . . . no pressure.

Go Time

Because the parole officer who'd be hearing my story was offsite, we'd all be on a video conference call. As we stepped into the room, I saw a five-inch by five-inch box on the monitor, displaying Phillip and Delores Robinson. The sight of them caused a lump to form in my throat. Accompanied by a victims' services advocate, Phillip and Mrs. Robinson had been given the opportunity to join us from an office in Nashville. Phillip and I had been corresponding for seven years, and this was to be the first time I'd seen him since the trial, when I had done everything I could to *not* see him. Now I was eager to see the man with whom I'd shared the deepest concerns of my heart.

Going into the hearing, I knew I had a few things going in my favor. For starters, I was a veteran. And also I'd been on my best behavior in prison during the seventeen years since I'd come to walk with Christ. I also had reason to believe that the Robinsons would put in a good word for me.

A tech guy from the prison fiddled on his laptop until the parole officer, named Mr. Gobble, in Cleveland, Tennessee, and the Robinsons were both visible onscreen. A part of me still couldn't understand their forgiveness, their love for God, or their love for me. I've never seen anyone who embodied love and compassion the way the Robinson family had. I fought back the tears that insisted on being expressed. This moment was too important for me to become undone by my overwhelming emotions. I willed myself to pull it together.

Mr. Gobble began by introducing himself, and asked me to begin by describing what happened on November 14, 1986. Although it had always been painful for me to think about that day, the difficulty of this telling was compounded because it was the first time I'd be telling the truth in front of the Robinsons.

I forced the words out, one by one, but I had difficulty speaking. I was very emotional as I described the day, and intermittently I'd apologize to Phillip and Mrs. Robinson for what I'd done.

At one point I looked down and noticed that I was digging my thumbnail under my fingernails to cause pain. It was as if the inner pain I could not bear had to be made manifest in my body.

When Mr. Gobble asked what led up to me taking Frank Wayne Robinson's life, I described how we'd met Monk and become obsessed with greed. When I described the gun exploding, I could see the victims' services advocate gently holding Mrs. Robinson's arm. Even as I was testifying, I was aware that I was jabbering on and saying all the wrong things. When I finished, I broke down weeping.

Scanning the various judgments and reports in my file, Mr. Gobble asked about my drug use in prison.

Solemnly, I told him the truth about my meth use. "When you take a man's life, that's all the rehab you need. That cured me."

He accepted my answer. When asked about my experience over the previous twenty-seven years, I was able to report that I'd been a diligent worker and upstanding prisoner. But just four weeks earlier, that sparkling-clean record had suddenly been put at risk. Knowing that I was up for parole and so would be unlikely to cause a commotion, another prisoner had messed with me in the chow hall, stealing my milk. At first, my temper flared, but I had buddies around me who reminded me that that guy wasn't worth it. Though we almost got into it, I was able to keep my cool.

Testimonies

Four of my family members spoke on my behalf. Because I'd been mentoring my grand-nephew with letters and phone calls, they shared my dedication to help children and confirmed that I'd have plenty of support at home upon my release. My mother expressed the regret and pain we all carry, and how deeply she hurt for the Robinson family.

One very special woman who testified on my behalf at the parole hearing was Carolyn Wilson. When her brother, a retired local school principal named Dan Wilson, had served as the principal of the prison vocational program, we'd become close friends. Dan and I had spent a lot of time discussing the Bible and the Lord. And during the course of our friendship he'd said, "Ron, I want to speak at your parole hearing, if that's okay. I've gotten to know what kind of person you are. I don't know if it'll help any, but I'd like to speak." When Dan's health deteriorated, and his kidneys were giving out, Carolyn wrote me a letter saying that if he was unable to do it, she'd like to speak at my hearing. Sadly, Dan had died four months earlier. I was so grateful that Carolyn, a circuit court clerk, had been so kind as to come and describe my relationship with her brother, and what she knew about me.

When Mr. Gobble gave the Robinsons a chance to speak, Mrs. Robinson spoke first. Because I'd always imagined her as a "victim," I'd expected her to be more . . . passive. So I was a bit surprised at how lively and forceful she was as she spoke.

She began, "I have forgiven Mr. Hammer. I think he is a different person today than he was twenty-seven years ago. He's moved on. I believe Mr. Hammer will do good if he's given the chance. It was my husband's life that he took, and I forgive him."

I knew I didn't deserve her generous words. But I received them as a gift from an amazing woman.

Mrs. Robinson continued, "I'd like to see him go home with his mama. To move on. To close this chapter."

Overwhelmed by her compassion and understanding, I felt my mother squeeze my hand. Then Phillip shared that he also believed in me and knew I was genuinely remorseful for my crime.

Finally, Mr. Gobble asked me why I should be granted parole. After blathering on to the Robinsons about how sorry I was, I let Mr. Gobble know that I'd discovered that helping others took some of my pain away. I told him how I'd tried to encourage the new guys coming into prison to stay away from gangs and drug use, inviting them to go to church with me. I always shared my story with these guys, admitting how I took a man's life in a split second because of my addiction. I was eager to keep telling my story in the hopes of preventing others from traveling the road I'd gone down. I said I'd moved on from the decisions I'd made as a young man and that, given the chance, I felt I could help people on the outside.

When our meeting ended, Mr. Gobble told us that he'd make his decision and would communicate it to the rest of the parole board for their approval. He would either recommend my release or suggest I stay in prison three more years. Although of course I wanted my freedom back, I can honestly say that I was prepared to serve three more years. I was able to experience that deep peace because I'd been set free in 2007 when Phillip Robinson sent me a letter forgiving me for killing his father. I can hear how unbelievable that sounds, but it's true.

After the screen went dark, I told my mom I wasn't sure I'd been able to communicate to Phillip and Mrs. Robinson the true remorse I felt in my heart. They had no way of knowing that not a day went by that I did not ask God to bless them. I'd always dreamed of seeing them in person, to express my remorse face to face, and I realized how difficult that would be emotionally.

That evening as I lay awake in bed yet another night, I made a personal oath to show God's kindness, love, and compassion to others to honor the Robinson family. More than anything I want to make sure that Wayne Robinson hadn't died in vain.

Five days later, I learned that the Tennessee Board of Parole voted for me to receive a psychological evaluation in Nashville, and that my next hearing would be in six months.

CHAPTER TWENTY-SIX

Time to Heal

Phillip, March 19, 2015

I don't know when they might get out, but I hope it's not before my mom dies."

For years the canned response had worked whenever someone asked when I thought Hammer and Kyger might be released. After their sentencing, a friend who was familiar with the criminal justice system had predicted that they'd serve thirty-five years, which would have sprung them free in 2022 when my mother was ninety-one years old. *If* she lived that long. It had always felt important to me that she be spared seeing their release in her lifetime, and I felt confident that—should they be released at that point—I'd be able to hide the truth from a ninety-one-year-old.

The system my mother had used to track Steve's and Ron's behavior in prison, the Felony Offender Information List, is what I began using in 2010 to track their parole eligibility dates. I watched helplessly as Ron's parole date had inched closer and closer.

Would I Speak for Ron?

As Ron marched toward eligibility, our relationship was growing and changing. I'd have to decide whether to stick by my original announcement that I wanted those "vermin" to rot in jail or whether I would speak in favor of Ron's parole with integrity. While both options were riddled with their own unique challenges, God had slowly been softening my heart toward Ron's release.

Not long after we'd received Ron's first letter, I'd participated in a mission trip, with my church, to Louisiana's Angola Prison. The maximum-security prison farm is the largest maximum-security prison in the United States, with 6,300 prisoners and 1,800 staff. The state execution chamber, for both men and women, is located at Angola. During our visit, prison warden Burl Cain spoke to us about the prison and about the mindset of prisoners. He acknowledged that when a man is incarcerated his loved ones begin to abandon him. His wife quits visiting and files for divorce. His children fade into silence. Close friends move on with their lives. The one person who sticks with a prisoner, through thick and thin, is his mother.

Cain explained, "Their mamas never leave them as long as they are alive."

So if a prisoner loses his mother while incarcerated, the loss can be devastating. Cain taught us that an inmate is typically the most unpredictable when his mother dies.

I'd been holding Cain's insight in my heart since that trip, especially as I learned more about Ron's relationship with his own mother. I'd even begun to imagine Ron having the opportunity to go home and care for her because I knew that Ron's greatest desire was to support his mom during the last years of her life. For the first time, with a new compassion in my heart for the Hammer family, I was able to imagine a world in which my mother was still living and Ron Hammer walked free.

Nashville Bound

My mother and I didn't know what to expect when we drove to Nashville to attend Ron's parole hearing. And, honestly, I didn't know what to expect from her. When I'd told her I was attending the hearing, I was surprised that she wanted to come with me. She'd been so cool toward him for years, and I wasn't sure where she stood at that point.

When we were about ten miles outside of the city, I asked, "So, do you just want to watch, or do you think you'd like to say anything?"

As if it had been the most foolish question in the world, she retorted, "I'll tell him I've forgiven him."

Although I'd seen her heart begin to change, it was the first time I'd heard her announce that she'd forgiven Ron. As I drove, I marveled at what God had done in her.

We'd been in touch with Tina Fox, the victims' service advocate, who'd been very kind to us. When we arrived at her office, she ushered us into a conference room with a monitor and chairs for the three of us. We had about ten minutes to wait until Ron joined the conference.

When we saw Ron on Ms. Fox's monitor, the first thing we noticed is that he'd aged. Of course we expected it, but our imaginations still relied heavily on the yellowing newspaper clippings that my mother had carefully clipped and placed in her scrapbook. Because Ron and I were about the same age, I'd experienced the same phenomena when I'd see old school friends. It was easy to see how they had aged, but I continued to see the same old guy in the mirror every morning.

Ms. Fox explained to us that Mr. Gobble would lead the meeting and described how she expected the hearing to unfold. When everyone was present, we acknowledged each other and began.

The hardest part of the hearing for my mother and me was hearing Ron describe the day of the murder. Because Steve and Ron had denied any involvement in the crime during the trial, there was no way for us to know what events had led up to my father's death. And by this point, we both had enough trust in Ron to believe that what he was saying was finally true. Already tortured for what he'd done, there was no more reason to lie.

Especially since he was taking more responsibility for the crime than what had been assumed during his trial.

Hearing that the plan to rob my father had originated with this new character, "Monk," spun a whole new twist in the plot on which we finally thought we had a good handle. But as Ron spoke, we learned that Monk had actually been the shady character who had been watching my father's routine and had generated the idea of robbing him at gunpoint. On one hand, it had been a kindness to us that Ron hadn't tried to shift blame from himself to anyone else. He'd taken full responsibility for his actions. On the other hand, it was very disturbing for my mother and I to learn that there was a third person complicit in my father's death.

At the end of the hearing, Mr. Gobble let us know that he'd voted in favor of Ron's release after completing a course designed to help with reentry and that we'd learn of the full board's decision within two weeks. And before signing off, he paused to speak directly to my mother and me.

"I can't believe you," he marveled. "I will never, never, never forget this hearing. I've never had one like it."

While it would have been easy for my mother and I to pat ourselves on the back, for our generosity of heart, I knew that what had happened between us had been a joint effort. Ron's courageous letter had been the accelerant to fuel the work God had been doing in all of our hearts. Without it, all three of us would still be limping wounded.

As my mother and I said goodbye to Tina Fox and left the government building, my mother commented, "I would love for everybody to have heard his story."

I understood what she meant. When she and I told others about the redemption God had been orchestrating, most were cautious in their response, fearing that Ron was deceiving us. That reserved judgment was something my mom's walking buddies at Stones River Mall had in common with guys on Ron's unit! Very few people had a holy imagination expansive enough to welcome and celebrate the miracle God was doing in our hearts. So my mother reasoned that if others experienced what we'd just experienced, if they could see what the Lord had done in Ron, they'd at last be able to understand.

Being present at Ron's hearing was a huge turning point for my mom. During the hearing, she had the opportunity to see Ron's sincerity, in his face and body and voice. As we discussed the hearing in the car on the drive home, she commented that he seemed like he was about to break down and cry during the entire proceeding. Witnessing his humanity moved my mom and her heart filled with love for the man she no longer referred to as "Hammer." As we drove home and processed all we'd heard and learned during the hearing, I recognized that she cared deeply for Ron.

Later that week we were informed that after Ron completed a psychological exam, he would have another hearing. Six months later, Mr. Gobble and a new board member heard Ron's case, and both voted for parole. Within the week, the other board members agreed.

Ron was going home.

CHAPTER TWENTY-SEVEN

A Traumatic Release

Ron; April 2, 2015

The morning I was scheduled to be released, I'd changed from my prison uniform into jeans and a button-down shirt. Anxious, waiting in a holding cell with others, gripping my release papers, I heard a corrections officer call four names.

To hear mine among them felt like a dream.

"Okay, guys," he hollered, "grab your trash and get out of my prison! You're no longer welcome here."

Hoping his was the last prison humor I'd be subject to, I grabbed my small bag of belongings and stood to leave. Rather than walk out the front door of the prison, we were directed to exit right and head out through the sally port. Because this was where all the supply trucks entered and exited the facility, security was extremely tight. Every vehicle entering or exiting was subject to a thorough investigation with a number of investigative devices including long poles with mirrors, to check underneath the vehicles, and even a heartbeat monitor.

Two large gates, one after the next, were controlled by an operator hidden behind mirrored glass. In order to best control vehicles coming and going, the two gates were never both open at the same time.

The other inmates and I had been allowed to pass through the first gate. Waiting in the sally port, my nerves were raw.

Two of the inmates were on foot and I was pushing a man named Mr. Williams in a wheelchair. As we waited my heart beat a little faster when I caught a glimpse of my mother waiting in the parking lot. Her hair was white and she was dressed in her Sunday church clothes.

As we stood in the center of the sally port, the corporal, from a doorway where he was watching our passage, shouted, "Hammer! Come here and have a seat! You're not going anywhere!"

Panicked, I returned to the bay where he was waiting and the hulking door closed behind so the other three prisoners could be released.

Any shred of hope I'd carried with me that morning drained from my body. I wanted only to collapse to the ground and break out in tears. Confused, my mind raced to figure out what had gone wrong. Dutiful, trying to remain calm, I showed the corporal my release papers. Uninterested, barely glancing at them, he had me locked up in a holding cell. Before returning to his office he told me to sit down and be patient. Though the instinct I'd developed over the years was to do exactly as I was told, I simply couldn't sit still. Instead, I walked several steps across the cell, and when I reached the other side I pivoted and walk in the other direction. Three steps east. Pivot. Three steps west.

His words continued to echo in my ears: *be patient.* With varying degrees of effectiveness, it's what I'd done for the last twenty-seven years and seven months. But something had shifted in my heart about eight years earlier. After Phillip and I had begun to correspond, he began sending me quotes, poems and other literature about patience. I'd taken each one to heart and purposed to grow in my faith. Phillip's friendship, and all I'd learned from his teachings, had transformed me into a different man than the terrified, addicted, lying one who'd been sentenced almost three decades earlier.

Taking a deep breath, I practiced patience.

But my mind kept returning to my mother. She had no idea why I'd been recalled. Thankfully, I'd been taught by my Savior to lean on him in times of trouble.

I just hadn't expected trouble to find me before I'd reached the parking lot.

Having no idea what could be wrong with my paperwork, I began to pray.

Release at Last

After fifteen minutes the Corporal opened the door of my cell and barked, "Okay, Hammer, let's go."

Standing outside the holding cell were four state maintenance employees I'd worked for over the last seventeen years that I'd been in prison at Mountain City, Tennessee. To my dismay, each one was grinning from ear to ear. They'd wanted to say goodbye to me and had set up the delay with the Corporal as a prank. It felt cruel. Thankfully there was now something more reliable than my circumstances at work inside me.

They'd all left the prison thousands of times, but this would be my first. As I said my goodbyes, I tried to be cordial, but was distracted. I could think of nothing other than getting out. Waving goodbye to the men who'd become friends, I passed once more through the first gate, through the sally port, and then past the second.

With tears streaming down her face, my mother held her arms open and received me. For years she'd trusted in Christ, praying and asking Him to change my heart. Because her steadfast faithfulness echoed with Christ's own faithfulness, I felt something of God's embrace as she wrapped her arms around me. In ways I couldn't quite explain, God had chosen to use his people—like my mother, like Phillip—to make Himself real to me. My mother's prayer that I would be set free, both physically and spiritually, was answered that day. Though I was now a fifty-seven-year-old man, when I put my arms around her I felt like the eight-year-old boy, who'd been lost in the woods, returning home to my mother.

Though her house, where we were headed, was four hours away, in Virginia, I was home.

My brothers had driven my mom down, and were also waiting beside her to scoop me up. But as I released my mother all I wanted to do was to get as far away from the prison as I could. Without even receiving their open-armed welcome, I rushed them into my brother's car and begged them to leave the awful place where I'd spent so many years and where I'd seen such horrors.

On the ride home I continually touched my clothes and my body to make sure I wasn't only *dreaming* that I was going home, as I'd dreamt for so many years.

When we pulled in the driveway of my mother's home I was again overcome with emotion. Looking up at the stars, I marveled at God's wonderful creation. It had been twenty-seven years and seven months since I'd seen the full expanse of their awesome beauty.

Hopping out and opening her door, I took my mother's arm and walked her into her home.

Every cell of my body was filled with emotion. Every moment felt foreign, but welcome: opening the door to the house, sitting on her couch, filling cups of water from the tap, falling into a bed without anyone monitoring my location.

Senses heightened, I lay awake for hours.

At around one in the morning I stood and began pacing. The guest bedroom my mother had prepared for me had just enough room for me to take three steps, from the hallway door to the closet, pivot, and take three steps back toward the door.

The familiar rhythm settled my soul.

During the hours I'd paced in my cell, I'd often dwell on God's love for me and God's love for others. Mile after mile behind bars, I was reminded that no pleasure or true happiness comes without knowing and loving our Savior. When all I wanted to do was rip open the gates of my cell and be free, the Lord taught me to be patient and trust him.

It's what I vowed, that night, to continue to do.

Cocooned

During those first months I wanted to stay by myself, as if nestled in God's presence. Though I didn't always understand why, I now believe that this was God's way of healing me deep inside my soul. It was a chance to humble myself before him and give him an abundance of praise for delivering me from prison and setting me free.

CHAPTER TWENTY-EIGHT

Brothers on a Mission

Phillip and Ron

Phillip

"I'm only here because of you," Ron gushed, as he hugged my mother.

Though they'd laid eyes on one another via teleconference, this was their first meeting in person. After driving eleven hours, we'd just pulled in the driveway of Ron's mother's home. Ron had hugged me when I'd gotten out of the car, and as my mother was emerging from the passenger's side, Ron was waiting to embrace her.

My mother said, with sincerity, "It's so good to finally meet you in person."

Susan, my mother, and I had driven north to Virginia to spend the Memorial Day weekend with Ron's family. He'd been released just seven weeks earlier. We had plans to speak at my church three weeks later, but it was unclear whether Ron's parole officer would allow him to leave the state. So we also had a video crew trailing us in another vehicle to film Ron, in case he wasn't able to be with us in Tennessee.

As we made our introductions in the driveway, competing emotions swelled within each of us.

Ron, who I'd learned rarely stays still for long, had been doing yard work for his mother. As he finished rolling up his orange extension cord, he invited us into the house to meet his mother. After introductions and hugs, those in our traveling crew used the restroom and gathered for cold drinks.

In the course of our correspondence, Ron and I had discovered that we were both runners. So before dinner, after our videographers had chatted with Ron, we both suited up in our running gear and went on a run together. The interview had been pretty emotional for Ron, and also for me, so it was good to be able to release some energy on the trail.

Hearing Ron describe, for the video, his attempts to take his own life was chilling. Because he is the most mechanically savvy person I know, it seemed like more than coincidence that each of his attempts, dependent on some sort of machinery, failed. It was one of many reminders that weekend that God had been orchestrating something greater than either of us had once imagined.

Morning Worship

After spending the night in a hotel in Harrisonburg, we met up with Ron at his church, where we were scheduled to share our story. Since his release, Ron had been a regular attender at a church where a childhood buddy of his was a pastor. The Shenandoah Assemblies of God church was a stately white tall-steeple building, as you might expect to see in the south. And while the sanctuary was lined with traditional pews, the service itself was very contemporary.

Although members of the congregation had seen Ron coming to worship with his mom, none knew his story. So they'd all showed up that morning expecting worship to look like it did every other Sunday.

After announcements, singing, and prayers, Pastor Carter Dean stood behind the pulpit to introduce us.

With a kind smile, he gently explained, "I've told y'all a little bit about me going to the parole hearing of a close friend I grew up with. Most folks call him Ron, but I call him Ronnie."

Folks in the congregation smiled.

"Because I wasn't quite sure how to approach this, I've kept this morning as a surprise for you. Ron has been worshiping with us recently, and today we have some special guests. Phillip Robinson is the son of Ron's victim, and his mother, Mrs. Robinson, was the victim's wife."

Glancing around, I could see that those who'd gathered didn't quite know how to respond.   Should they be happy? Scared? Angry? They continued to look to their pastor for emotional cues.

"The Robinson family traveled eleven hours to be with us this morning. And I think their story of forgiveness, that's touched me, is really going to touch you. So without further ado . . ."

Ron and I rose and walked to the front of the sanctuary. It was the first time we'd stood shoulder to shoulder to share our story. We had a rough outline of what we'd share, and exchanged the microphone a few times as our story unfolded. As Ron spoke, I saw eyes widen and jaws drop.

After Ron had shared with the congregation about his attempts to end his life, he handed the microphone to me.

"You weren't the only one who wanted you dead," I quipped, "I wanted you dead, too."

Again, the congregation was silent, unsure whether to laugh or cry.

What I most wanted them to recognize were echoes of Joseph's words to his brothers, in Egypt. After they'd left him for dead, and after he'd served years in prison for a crime he hadn't committed, and had eventually served as Pharaoh's right hand man, Joseph recognized divine *meaning* in the tragedy he'd endured.

When his brothers fell facedown before him, Joseph offered this gracious insight into God's divine plan that would yield good both for him and for them: "As for you, you meant evil against me, but God meant it for good, to bring it about that many people should be kept alive, as they are today" (Genesis 50:20, ESV). In spite of their thoughtless malicious act, God had wrought good from evil. And just as God had done it for Joseph, Ron and I were seeing and expecting God to do the same for us and for those who might be kept alive, or resurrected, through our story.

After the service, crowds lined up to greet us. Most were interested in speaking to my mother to ask how on earth she was ever able to forgive Ron. Smiling, knowing it was not by her own might, she gently acknowledged God's patient grace that had been at work in all of our hearts. A lot of those who spoke to us mentioned someone in their lives they knew they needed to forgive. A father. A sister. An ex-husband. It was particularly gratifying when someone would share that God had shown them what their next action step was in making those broken relationships right. It felt as if we were already seeing how what the enemy had meant for evil was being transformed, by God, for good.

Although we were feeling spent after the first service, as well as a bit naked, we were also scheduled to speak at the church's second service. We'd heard reports that people who'd attended the first service were calling family and friends who hadn't been at church to ensure that they came to the second service!

After another receiving line after the second service, folks eventually trickled away. With a long drive ahead of us, we headed toward the parking lot for the drive back to Tennessee.

When we'd arrived the day before, Susan had been a bit aloof around Ron. She wasn't rude, but she'd always felt like being in relationship with Ron was "my" thing and not her thing. And Ron surely felt the cool chill she was giving off.

As we chatted briefly beside the car before we left, I noticed Susan had a smile on her face I'd not seen before when we'd discussed Ron or during the hours we'd spent with him.

After giving Ron an obligatory hug goodbye, she looked him the eye and explained, "I thought this was Phillip's thing, and I wasn't totally for it."

She continued, "But this weekend has shed a different light on things for me. I see there is something very powerful here, and I want you to know that I forgive you, too."

Ron's eyes filled with gratitude. "Thank you so much," he eked out, reaching for a second hug. "I'm so sorry for putting you all through what I've put you through. I apologize with all my heart."

As was so often the case, his genuine remorse was palpable.

As Susan slipped into the car, she assured him, "It's all going to be alright."

And it is.

Ron

Phillip's church had appealed to my parole officer to let me visit his church in Murfreesboro, New Vision, so that we could tell our story in Sunday morning worship. That service was scheduled just three weeks after we'd spoken at my church. She denied the request. But eventually, with a good bit of resistance during the request process, she allowed Sharon and me to drive to Tennessee October 23, 2015. New Vision was hosting a day-long conference for local prisoners, called Redeemed for Life. Inmates from a minimum-security work center were granted supervised release for the day, and their families were also invited. After music and speakers in the sanctuary, families could share a meal together.

Sharon and I had remarried three weeks earlier. I'd actually wanted Phillip to perform the ceremony, but since Sharon had not yet met Phillip, she had some reservations about it. She also didn't know how we'd be accepted back in Murfreesboro. Respecting her wishes, we were married by my pastor in a simple ceremony in my church.

So Sharon and I were feeling a little bit like giddy newlyweds on the world's weirdest honeymoon. We checked into the Hilton, where the church had reserved us a room, and were treated like royalty there. Although Sharon had continued to live in Tennessee for eleven years after I'd been incarcerated, it was my first trip back to Tennessee as a free man. As we approached town, the geography and familiar sights brought up a lot of emotion for me.

We planned to meet Phillip at New Vision, but had arrived in town with time to cruise around after we'd checked in at the hotel. I was surprised to see the development that had happened in thirty years. The house Sharon and I had been so proud to purchase looked the same. My shop was now a truck accessory store called Truck Accents. We drove past the IGA parking lot in silence.

Because Sharon hadn't spent time with Phillip when he'd traveled to Virginia, I was thrilled for her to meet him. After giving us a tour of the church, we met Susan and Phillip's mother at the Chop House for dinner together. After the meal, I was dying to hear what Sharon would think of the Robinsons.

As we drove back to the hotel in our Honda rental car I pressed her for a report.

"I don't know what to say. I guess I can't believe that Susan and Delores treated me like . . . a sister. I felt like I was part of the family."

Redeemed for Life

The next morning we arrived at the conference bright and early. Phillip and I were on a panel together, and we also got to hear other speakers. Six inmates were baptized during the worship time.

After the program, prisoners were securely ushered from the worship center to the church's student center where tables were set for the meal.

When everyone had found their seats at the tables, one of the conference organizers stood up with a microphone and began to speak about Sharon and me. She shared that we'd been childhood sweethearts since third grade and had been married twenty-six years, before divorcing while I was in prison. Six years later, she explained, we'd remarried. She said the Redeemed for Life team knew we hadn't had a proper wedding reception, and that they wanted to give us one. Then she invited Sharon and I up to cut a beautiful tiered wedding cake they'd provided. Photographers were ready for the photo op, like they had been at our first wedding!

As the room erupted into applause, Sharon and I both teared up. Our own families hadn't organized a reception for us, and these strangers wanted to celebrate with us. We were both deeply moved by the kindness.

Running Together

Saturday afternoon, Phillip, his son Nathaniel, and I met at a local trail to take a run together. After we stretched and started our run, I began to hear echoes, in my head, of voices of guys with whom I'd been in prison: the ones who, like Steve, had been suspect of Phillip's intentions when he wrote to say he'd forgiven me. And, like them, my mindset, too, had been formed in prison. As we ran, I began to wonder why Phillip had brought along his muscled-up two-hundred-pound son. I was careful to keep Nathaniel in front of me so I could keep an eye on him.

Around mile number six, Nathaniel was getting winded.

"Well," he heaved, "I'm gonna walk."

Alarm bells went off in my mind. The fact that they'd split up concerned me. Although I kept pace with Phillip, I kept checking behind me, rubbernecking, to keep an eye on Nathaniel. I finally relaxed a bit when I saw Nathaniel fade out of view.

Toward the end of our route, Phillip and I slowed to a walk until Nathaniel caught up with us. My instinctive vigilance kicked back in.

Near the end of our run, we were running alongside the Stones River, in the exact spot I'd followed to reach my shop after our crime. Although I hadn't mentioned my concerns about being harmed by Phillip and Nathaniel, knowing at some level that they could be trusted, I ended up telling them how my fellow inmates had believed Phillip wanted to harm me.

As if planned, both of them broke out in an evil cackle, pretending they were filled with malicious intent.

"Yes," chimed Nathaniel, "we're actually here to drown you."

When they both started laughing, I finally let down my guard and joined them.

Back at the IGA

Because we'd parked not far from the old IGA supermarket, now a hardware store, we'd agreed to visit that holy ground together before I showered up and drove home with Sharon.

As we slowly approached the store, I noticed that Phillip and I began to diverge ways. He was heading toward a spot near the store, where he'd watched paramedics fighting to save his father's life. I was heading toward the parking spot where I'd first seen Wayne Robinson emerge from his vehicle.

Phillip pointed to a spot on the ground he'd eyeballed from the vantage point of hanging on to a pole for support as he watched his mother crouched beside his father's body.

"Dad was here," he reported.

From about thirty feet away I corrected, "No, it happened here."

I felt a familiar wave of emotion sweep through my body. Gulping deep breaths of air, I willed myself to hold it together in front of Phillip and Nathaniel.

"I was skin and bones," I explained, "and your dad tossed me about a bit. He was pretty strong. A big guy."

Phillip and Nathaniel nodded solemnly.

"It was a real struggle," I told them. "He grabbed my shoulder and I was trying to get away from his grasp. I'm sure he smelled liquor on my breath. He just knew I was an old drunk."

I second-guessed whether I should be reporting what I remembered, but both men seemed willing and eager to hear.

"As I tried to get away," I explained, "he grabbed my shoulder. We were right here. Then, it was like time stopped. As I tried to get away, he grabbed the gun from me . . ."

As a customer exited the hardware store, passed us, and returned to his car, the three of us stood together in silence. Because no words could do justice to the sacred moment, silence was right.

After a few minutes, Phillip offered, "Let's pray."

Bowing our heads, we joined hands in a small circle to mark the moment and the space as sacred. The vulnerability of closing our eyes together reminded me that we'd truly begun to trust one another.

"Father, we praise you. We are here because of you, God, and the supernatural power of forgiveness. And we believe we are part of a story that is not ours, but yours," Phillip began. He continued to pray, asking that his father's death not be in vain.

I added, "Lord, we want to honor Wayne Robinson and we want to glorify you. Equip us to be your servants and to share the story of your forgiveness and redemption."

Phillip added, "Father, we believe that what man intended for evil, you intended for good. We give ourselves to you and ask that you would use our story to point others to the full life that is found only in you."

And together, with tears streaming down our faces, we all chimed, in unison, "Amen."

FINDING FREEDOM IN YOUR OWN STORY

*"When we forgive, we bring in light where there was darkness.
We open the door to an unseen future that our painful past had shut.
When we forgive, we take God's hand, walk through the door,
and stroll into possibilities that wait for us to make them real."*
- Lewis Smedes

What would happen if you came out of hiding to tell your story? Your story of being stuck in unforgiveness, but desiring freedom. Your story of forgiving. Your story of being forgiven. Are you curious to know how your life can be transformed when you embrace forgiveness?

We are convinced that all of us participate in the good God has for us, giving God access to do great things in our lives, by agreeing to forgive and be forgiven. Not only have we experienced this in our own lives, but as we've shared our story with audiences we've heard from countless others who are experiencing God's goodness by saying "yes" to forgiveness.

Ephesians 3:20 promises that God can do more than we can ask or imagine, and we believe God wants to do more in your life than you've dreamed possible. That's why we want to hear and share your story of offering or receiving forgiveness. If you've never shared it before, or if you've told everyone you know, we want to hear how forgiveness has changed you.

Join us by sharing your story at www.forgivenessjourneys.com or write to us at Forgiveness Journeys, PO Box 12091, Murfreesboro, TN 37129.

To God be the glory,
Ron and Phillip

ABOUT THE PUBLISHER

FH Publishers is a division of FaithHappenings.com

FaithHappenings.com is the premier, first-of-its kind, online Christian resource that contains an array of valuable local and national faith-based information all in one place. Our mission is "to inform, enrich, inspire and mobilize Christians and churches while enhancing the unity of the local Christian community so they can better serve the needs of the people around them." FaithHappenings.com will be the primary i-Phone, Droid App/Site and website that people with a traditional Trinitarian theology will turn to for national and local information to impact virtually every area of life.

The vision of FaithHappenings.com is to build the vibrancy of the local church with a true "one-stop-resource" of information and events that will enrich the soul, marriage, family, and church life for people of faith. We want people to be touched by God's Kingdom, so they can touch others FOR the Kingdom.

Find out more at www.faithhappenings.com.